OCCULT GLOSSARY

BY THE SAME AUTHOR

The Dialogues of G. de Purucker
The Esoteric Tradition
Fountain-Source of Occultism
The Four Sacred Seasons
Fundamentals of the Esoteric Philosophy
Golden Precepts of Esotericism
Man in Evolution
Messages to Conventions
The Path of Compassion
Questions We All Ask
The Story of Jesus
Studies in Occult Philosophy
Wind of the Spirit

Occult Glossary

A COMPENDIUM OF ORIENTAL AND THEOSOPHICAL TERMS

G. de PURUCKER

THEOSOPHICAL UNIVERSITY PRESS
PASADENA, CALIFORNIA

THEOSOPHICAL UNIVERSITY PRESS
POST OFFICE BOX C
PASADENA, CALIFORNIA 91109-7107
1996

Second and Revised Edition

First Edition published by Rider & Co., London, 1933

∞
The paper in this book meets the standards for permanence and durability of the Council on Library Resources.

Library of Congress Cataloging-in-Publication Data

Purucker, G. de (Gottfried), 1874-1942.
Occult glossary : a compendium of Oriental and theosophical terms / G. de Purucker. — 2nd & rev. ed.
p. cm.
Includes index.
ISBN 1-55700-050-6 (cloth : alk. paper)
ISBN 1-55700-051-4 (paper : alk. paper)

1. Theosophy—Dictionaries. I. Title.

BP527.P8 1996
299′.934′03—dc20 96-41435
CIP

Printed at Theosophical University Press
Pasadena, California

Publisher's Note

Every branch of study has its own special terminology, and the esoteric philosophies are no exception. This compendium not only clarifies the significance of the terms most frequently found in such literature, but offers a comprehensive outline of the scope and principles underlying an age-old tradition respecting the constitution of man and the universe in which he lives.

This Second and Revised Edition is faithful to the original 1933 edition. Changes include modernizing capitalization, spelling, and punctuation, and amending a few foreign terms (with appreciation to Dr. Bruce C. Hall and Mr. David Reigle for their respective contributions). The index has also been enlarged.

Key to the Pronunciation of Sanskrit Words

Sanskrit transliteration follows the modern system, except for the following letters to facilitate pronunciation: c = ch, ch = chh, ṛ = ṛi, ṣ = sh

a	as in org*a*n (not the a in man)	Example:	l*a*ya
ā	f*a*r (not the a in hat)		*ā*tman
ai	*ai*sle (not the ai in stain)		t*ai*jasa
au	h*ow* (not the au in haul)		bh*au*mika
b	ru*b*		*B*rahmā
bh	ru*b-h*ard		*bh*ūta
ch	*ch*air (not the k-sound as in can)		*ch*akra
chh	staun*ch-h*earted		*chh*āyā
d	*D*avid		*d*eva
dh	sa*d-h*earted		*dh*arma
dhy	the "dh" as above, but pronounce as though a "y" were added after the "h" — "sa*d-hy*earted" (not j as in John)		*dhy*āna
e	th*ey* (not e as in then or these)		d*e*va
g	*g*o (not as in legion)		*g*uru
h	*h*arm		*h*ari
i	p*i*n		p*i*tṛi
ī	pol*i*ce		av*ī*chi
j	*j*oy (not as in azure)		*j*īva
jñ	ca*ny*on (*j* is silent)		*jñ*āna (pronounced *nyāna*)
k	*k*elp		*k*alpa
l	*l*et		*l*aya
m	*m*an		*m*anas
n	*n*ature		*n*irvāṇa

ñ	ca*ny*on	j*ñ*āna
ṅg	fi*ng*er (not as in thing)	li*ṅg*a-śarīra
o	*g*o (not as in got)	b*o*dhi
p	*p*ath	*p*ralaya
ph	u*ph*ill (not as in sapphire)	*ph*ala
r	*r*ose	*r*ajas
s	le*ss*on (not as in rose)	*s*at
ś	*sh*ear	*ś*arīra
sh	ru*sh* (not as in pleasure)	śi*sh*ṭa
t	*t*ub	*t*amas
th	ligh*t-h*earted (not as in then)	s*th*ūla
u	p*u*ll (not as in union)	*u*panishad
ū	r*u*le (not as in view)	bh*ū*ta
v	*v*oice (may be pronounced as a *w* after a consonant)	*v*idyā, svapna
y	*y*et	*y*ogin

Note — When several consonants come together, do not pronounce by inserting vowels between them: thus, ksha-tri-ya (not ke-shat-u-ri-ya), bhak-ti (not buh-hak-ti).

Accentuation: Syllables are either *heavy* or *light*. Heavy syllables contain either a long vowel, or a short vowel followed by two or more consonants (aspirated letters such as *bh* are single consonants). Generally, the stress falls on the heavy syllable closest to the end of a word but not the last syllable. Examples: tu-**rī**-ya, man-**van**-ta-ra, pra-**jā**-pa-ti; but u-pa-ni-shad (which has no heavy syllable).

The *ṛ*, *ṇ*, and *ṭ*, (as in prak*ṛ*iti, Brāhma*ṇ*a, and śish*ṭ*a), though necessary to the correct transliteration of the Sanskrit, and somewhat affecting the pronunciation, may be ignored for practical purposes.

The *dz* combination (as in *Dz*yan) is not Sanskrit, but should be pronounced as in a*dz*e (not j as in John).

Additional help in pronouncing Sanskrit terms, with recorded examples, may be found in *Sanskrit Pronunciation: Booklet and Cassette* by Bruce Cameron Hall, Theosophical University Press, 1992.

OCCULT GLOSSARY

Occult Glossary

A Compendium of Oriental and Theosophical Terms

Absolute A term which unfortunately is much abused and often misused even in theosophical writings. It is a convenient word in Occidental philosophy by which is described the utterly unconditioned; but it is a practice which violates both the etymology of the word and even the usage of some keen and careful thinkers as, for instance, Sir William Hamilton in his *Discussions* (3rd edition, page 13, footnote), who apparently uses the word *absolute* in the exactly correct sense in which theosophists should use it as meaning "finished," "perfected," "completed." As Hamilton observes: "The *Absolute* is diametrically opposed to, is contradictory of, the Infinite" (q.v.). This last statement is correct, and in careful theosophical writings the word Absolute should be used in Hamilton's sense, as meaning that which is freed, unloosed, perfected, completed.

Absolute is from the Latin *absolutum,* meaning "freed," "unloosed," and is, therefore, an exact English parallel of the Sanskrit philosophical term *moksha* or *mukti*, and more mystically of the Sanskrit term so commonly found in Buddhist writings especially, *nirvāṇa* — an extremely profound and mystical thought.

Hence, to speak of parabrahman as being the Absolute may be a convenient usage for Occidentals who understand neither the significance of the term parabrahman nor the etymology, origin, and proper usage of the English word Absolute — "proper" outside of a common and familiar employment.

In strict accuracy, therefore, the student should use the word Absolute only when he means what the Hindu philosopher means when he speaks of moksha or mukti or of a mukta — i.e., one who has obtained mukti or freedom, one who has arrived at the acme or summit of all evolution possible in any one hierarchy, although as compared with hierarchies still more sublime, such jīvanmukta is but a mere beginner. The Silent Watcher in theosophical philosophy is an outstanding example of one who can be said to be absolute in the fully accurate meaning of the word. It is obvious that the Silent Watcher is not parabrahman. (*See also* MOKSHA, RELATIVITY)

Adept The word means one who is "skilled"; hence, even in our ordinary life, a chemist, a physician, a theologian, a mechanic, an engineer, a teacher of languages, an astronomer, are all "adepts," persons who are skilled, each in his own profession. In theosophical writings, however, an Adept is one who is skilled in the esoteric wisdom, in the teachings of life.

Ādi-Buddhi *See* SVABHAVAT

Advaita-Vedanta *See* VEDĀNTA

Agnishvātta(s) (Sanskrit) A compound of two words: *agni*, "fire"; *shvātta*, "tasted" or "sweetened," from *svad*, verb-root meaning "to taste" or "to sweeten." Therefore, literally one who has been delighted or sweetened by fire. A class of pitṛis: our solar ancestors as contrasted with the barhishads, our lunar ancestors.

The kumāras, agnishvāttas, and mānasaputras are three groups or aspects of the same beings: the kumāras represent the aspect of original spiritual purity untouched by gross elements of matter. The agnishvāttas represent the aspect of their connection with the sun or solar spiritual fire. Having tasted or been "sweetened" by the spiritual fire — the fire of intellectuality and spirituality — they have been purified thereby. The mānasaputras represent the aspect of intellectuality — the functions of higher intellect.

The agnishvāttas and mānasaputras are two names for the same class or host of beings, and set forth or signify or represent two different aspects or activities of this one class of beings. Thus, for instance, a man may be said to be a kumāra in his spiritual parts, an agnishvātta in his buddhic-mānasic parts, and a mānasaputra in his purely mānasic aspect. Other beings could be called kumāras in their highest aspects, as for instance the beasts, but they are not imbodied agnishvāttas or mānasaputras.

The agnishvāttas are the solar spiritual-intellectual parts of us, and therefore are our inner teachers. In preceding manvantaras, they had completed their evolution in the realms of physical matter, and when the evolution of lower beings had brought these latter to the proper state, the agnishvāttas came to the rescue of these who had only the physical "creative fire," thus inspiring and enlightening these lower lunar pitṛis with spiritual and intellectual energies or "fires."

When this earth's planetary chain shall have reached the end of its seventh round, we, as then having completed the evolutionary course for this planetary chain, will leave this planetary chain as dhyān-chohans, agnishvāttas; but the others now trailing along behind us — the present beasts — will be the lunar pitṛis of the next planetary chain to come.

While it is correct to say that these three names appertain to the same class of beings, nevertheless each name has its own significance in the occult teaching, which is why the three names are used with three distinct meanings. Imagine an unconscious god-spark beginning its evolution in any one solar or mahā-manvantara. We may call it a kumāra, a being of original spiritual purity, but with a destiny through karmic evolution connected with the realms of matter.

At the other end of the line, at the consummation of the evolution in this mahā-manvantara, when the evolving entity has become a fully self-conscious god or divinity, its proper appellation then is agnishvātta, for it has been "sweetened" or purified by means of the working through it of the spiritual fires inherent in itself.

Now then, when such an agnishvātta assumes the role of a bringer of mind or of intellectual light to a lunar pitṛi which it overshadows and in which a ray from it incarnates, it then, although in its own realm an agnishvātta, functions as a mānasaputra or child of mind or mahat. A brief analysis of the compound elements of these three names may be useful.

Kumāra is from *ku* meaning "with difficulty" and *māra* meaning "mortal." The significance of the word therefore can be paraphrased as "mortal with difficulty," and the meaning usually given to it by Sanskrit scholars as "easily dying" is wholly exoteric and amusing, and doubtless arose from the fact that kumāra is a word frequently used for child or boy, everybody knowing that young children "die easily." The idea therefore is that purely spiritual beings, although ultimately destined by evolution to pass through the realms of matter, become mortal, i.e., material, only with difficulty.

Agnishvātta has the meaning stated above, "delighted" or "pleased" or "sweetened," i.e., "purified" by fire — which we may render in two ways: either as the fire of suffering and pain in material existence producing great fiber and strength of character, i.e., spirituality; or, perhaps still better from the standpoint of occultism, as signifying an entity or entities who have become one in essence through evolution with the aethery fire of spirit.

Mānasaputra is a compound of two words: *mānasa*, "mental" or "intellectual," from the word *manas*, "mind," and *putra*, "son" or "child," therefore a child of the cosmic mind — a "mind-born son" as H. P. Blavatsky phrases it. (*See also* Pitṛis, Lunar Pitṛis)

Ahaṅkāra (Sanskrit) A compound word: *aham*, "I"; *kāra*, "maker" or "doer," from the verb-root *kṛi*, "to do," "to make"; egoism, personality. The egoistical and māyāvi principle in man, born of the ignorance or avidyā which produces the notion of the "I" as being different from the universal One-Self.

Ākāśa (Sanskrit) The word means "brilliant," "shining," "luminous." The fifth kosmic element, the fifth essence or "quintessence," called Aether by the ancient Stoics; but it is not the ether of science. The ether of science is merely one of its lower elements. In the Brahmanical scriptures ākāśa is used for what the northern Buddhists call svabhavat, more mystically Ādi-buddhi — "primeval buddhi"; it is also mūlaprakṛiti, the kosmical spirit-substance, the reservoir of Being and of beings. The Hebrew Old Testament refers to it as the kosmic "waters." It is universal substantial *space*; also mystically Alaya. (*See also* MŪLAPRAKṚITI, ALAYA)

Alaya (Sanskrit) A compound word: *a*, "not"; *laya*, from the verb-root *lī*, "to dissolve"; hence "the indissoluble." The universal soul; the basis or root or fountain of all beings and things — the universe, gods, monads, atoms, etc. Mystically identical with ākāśa in the latter's highest elements, and with mūlaprakṛiti in the latter's essence as "root-producer" or "root-nature." (*See also* ĀKĀŚA, BUDDHI, MŪLAPRAKṚITI)

[NOTE: *The Secret Doctrine* (I:49) mentions Alaya in the Yogāchāra system, most probably referring to *ālaya-vijñāna*, but adds that with the "Esoteric 'Buddhists' . . . 'Alaya' has a double and even a triple meaning." — PUBLISHER]

Ānanda *See* SAT

Antaskaraṇa (Sanskrit) Perhaps better spelled as antaḥkaraṇa. A compound word: *antar*, "interior," "within"; *karaṇa*, sense organ. Occultists explain this word as the bridge between the higher and lower manas or between the spiritual ego and *personal* soul of man. Such is H. P. Blavatsky's definition. As a matter of fact there are several antaḥkaraṇas in the human septenary constitution — one for every *path* or *bridge* between any two of the several monadic centers in man. Man is a microcosm, therefore a unified composite, a unity in diversity; and the antaḥkaraṇas are the links of vibrating consciousness-substance uniting these various centers.

Anupapādaka *See* AUPAPĀDUKA

Arūpa (Sanskrit) A compound word meaning "formless," but this word formless is not to be taken so strictly as to mean that there is no form of any kind whatsoever; it merely means that the forms in the spiritual worlds (the arūpa-lokas) are of a spiritual type or character, and of course far more ethereal than are the forms of the rūpa-lokas.

Thus in the arūpa-lokas, or the spiritual worlds or spheres or planes, the vehicle or body of an entity is to be conceived of rather as an enclosing sheath of energic substance. We can conceive of an entity whose form or body is entirely of electrical substance — as indeed our own bodies are in the last analysis of modern science. But such an entity with an electrical body, although distinctly belonging to the rūpa worlds, and to one of the lowest rūpa worlds, would merely, by comparison with our own gross physical bodies, seem to us to be bodiless or formless. (*See also* Rūpa, Loka)

Āsana (Sanskrit) A word derived from the verbal root *ās*, signifying "to sit quietly." Āsana, therefore, technically signifies one of the peculiar postures adopted by Hindu ascetics, mostly of the haṭha yoga school. Five of these postures are usually enumerated, but nearly ninety have been noted by students of the subject. A great deal of quasi-magical and mystical literature may be found devoted to these various postures and collateral topics, and their supposed or actual psychological value when assumed by devotees; but, as a matter of fact, a great deal of this writing is superficial and has very little indeed to do with the actual occult and esoteric training of genuine occultists. One is instinctively reminded of other quasi-mystical practices, as, for instance, certain genuflections or postures followed in the worship of the Christian Church, to which particular values are sometimes ascribed by fanatic devotees.

Providing that the position of the body be comfortable so that the mind is least distracted, genuine meditation and spiritual and actual introspection can be readily and successfully attained by any earnest student without the slightest attention being paid to these various postures. A man sitting quietly in his armchair, or lying in his bed at night, or sitting or lying on the grass in a forest, can more readily enter the inner worlds than by adopting and following any one or more of these various āsanas, which at the best are physiological aids of relatively small value. (*See also* SAMĀDHI)

Asat (Sanskrit) A term meaning the "unreal" or the manifested universe; in contrast with sat (q.v.), the real. In another and even more mystical sense, asat means even beyond or higher than sat, and therefore asat — "not sat." In this significance, which is profoundly occult and deeply mystical, asat really signifies the unevolved or rather unmanifested nature of parabrahman — far higher than sat, which is the reality of manifested existence.

Ascending Arc or **Luminous Arc** This term, as employed in theosophical occultism, signifies the passage of the life-waves or life-streams of evolving monads upwards along, on, and through the globes of the chain of any celestial body, the earth's chain included. Every celestial body (including the earth) is one member in a limited series or group of globes. These globes exist on different kosmic planes in a rising series. The life-waves or life-streams during any manvantara of such a chain circle or cycle around these globes in periodical surges or impulses. The ascent from the physical globe upwards is called the ascending arc; the descent through the more spiritual and ethereal globes downwards to the physical globe is called the descending arc. (*See also* PLANETARY CHAIN)

Āśrama (Sanskrit) A word derived from the root *śram*, signifying "to make efforts," "to strive"; with the particle *ā*, which in this case gives force to the verbal root *śram*. Āśrama has at least two main significations. The first is that of a college or school or a hermitage, an abode of ascetics, etc.; whereas the second meaning signifies a period of effort or striving in the religious life or career of a Brāhmaṇa of olden days. These periods of life in ancient times in Hindustan were four in number: the first, that of the student or brahmachārin; second, the period of life called that of the gṛihastha or householder — the period of married existence when the Brāhmaṇa took his due part in the affairs of men, etc.; third, the vānaprastha, or period of monastic seclusion, usually passed in a vana, or wood or forest, for purposes of inner recollection and spiritual meditation; and fourth, that of the bhikshu or religious mendicant, meaning one who has completely renounced the distractions of worldly life and has turned his attention wholly to spiritual affairs.

Brahmāśrama. In modern esoteric or occult literature, the compound term Brahmāśrama is occasionally used to signify an initiation chamber or secret room or adytum where the initiant or neophyte is striving or making efforts to attain union with Brahman or the inner god.

Astral Body This is the popular term for the model-body, the liṅga-śarīra (q.v.). It is but slightly less material than is the physical body, and is in fact the model or framework around which the physical body is builded, and from which, in a sense, the physical body flows or develops as growth proceeds. It is the vehicle of prāṇa or life-energy, and is, therefore, the container of all the energies descending from the higher parts of the human constitution by means of the prāṇic stream. The astral body precedes in time the physical body, and is the pattern around which the physical body is slavishly molded, atom by atom. In one sense the physical body may be called the deposit or dregs or lees of the astral body; the astral body likewise in its turn is but a deposit from the auric egg (q.v.).

Astral Light The astral light corresponds in the case of our globe, and analogically in the case of our solar system, to what the liṅga-śarīra (q.v.) is in the case of an individual man. Just as in man the liṅga-śarīra or astral body is the vehicle or carrier of prāna or life-energy, so is the astral light the carrier of the cosmic jīva (q.v.) or cosmic life-energy. To us humans it is an invisible region surrounding our earth, as H. P. Blavatsky expresses it, as indeed it surrounds every other physical globe; and among the seven kosmic principles it is the most material excepting one, our physical universe.

The astral light therefore is, on the one hand, the storehouse or repository of all the energies of the kosmos on their way downwards to manifest in the material spheres — of our solar system in general as well as of our globe in particular; and, on the other hand, it is the receptacle or magazine of whatever passes out of the physical sphere on its upward way.

Thirdly, it is a kosmic "picture-gallery" or indelible record of whatever takes place on the astral and physical planes; however, this last phase of the functions of the astral light is the least in importance and real interest.

The astral light of our own globe, and analogically of any other physical globe, is the region of the kāma-loka (q.v.), at least as concerns the intermediate and lower parts of the kāma-loka; and all entities that die pass through the astral light on their way upwards, and in the astral light throw off or shed the kāma-rūpa (q.v.) at the time of the second death.

The solar system has its own astral light in general, just as every globe in the universal solar system has its astral light in particular, in each of these last cases being a thickening or materializing or concreting around the globe of the general astral substance forming the astral light of the solar system. The astral light, strictly speaking, is simply the lees or dregs of ākāśa and exists in steps or stages of increasing ethereality. The more closely it surrounds any globe, the grosser and more material it is. It is the receptacle of all the vile and horrible emanations from earth and earth beings, and is therefore in parts filled with earthly pollutions. There is a constant interchange, unceasing throughout the solar manvantara, between the astral light on the one hand, and our globe earth on the other, each giving and returning to the other.

Finally, the astral light is with regard to the material realms of the solar system the copy or reflection of what the ākāśa is in the spiritual realms. The astral light is the mother of the physical, just as the spirit is the mother of the ākāśa; or, inversely, the physical is merely the concretion of the astral, just as the ākāśa is the veil or concretion of the highest spiritual. Indeed, the astral and physical are one, just as the ākāśic and the spiritual are one.

Astrology The astrology of the ancients was indeed a great and noble science. It is a term which means the "science of the celestial bodies." Modern astrology is but the tattered and rejected outer coating of real, ancient astrology; for that truly sublime science was the doctrine of the origin, of the nature, of the being, and of the destiny of the solar bodies, of the planetary bodies, and of the beings who dwell on them. It also taught the science of the relations of the parts of kosmic nature among themselves, and more particularly as applied to man and his destiny as forecast by the celestial orbs. From that great and noble science sprang up an exoteric pseudo-science, derived from the Mediterranean and Asian practice, eventuating in the modern scheme called astrology — a tattered remnant of ancient wisdom.

In actual fact, genuine archaic astrology was one of the branches of the ancient Mysteries, and was studied to perfection in the ancient Mystery schools. It had throughout all ancient time the unqualified approval and devotion of the noblest men and of the greatest sages. Instead of limiting itself as modern so-called astrology does to a system based practically entirely upon certain branches of mathematics, in archaic days the main body of doctrine which astrology then contained was transcendental metaphysics, dealing with the greatest and most abstruse problems concerning the universe and man. The celestial bodies of the physical universe were considered in the archaic astrology to be not merely time markers, or to have vague relations of a psychomagnetic quality as among themselves — although indeed this is true — but to be the vehicles of starry spirits, bright and living gods, whose very existence and characteristics, individually as well as collectively, made them the governors and expositors of destiny.

Aśvattha (Sanskrit) The mystical tree of knowledge, the mystical tree of kosmical life and being, represented as growing in a reversed position: the branches extending downwards and the roots upwards. The branches typify the visible kosmical universe, the roots the invisible world of spirit.

The universe among the ancients of many nations was portrayed or figurated under the symbol of a tree, of which the roots sprang from the divine heart of things, and the trunk and the branches and the branchlets and the leaves were the various planes and worlds and spheres of the kosmos. The fruit of this kosmic tree contained the seeds of future "trees," being the entities which had attained through evolution the end of their evolutionary journey, such as men and the gods — themselves universes in the small, and destined in the future to become kosmic entities when the cycling wheel of time shall have turned through long aeons on its majestic round. In fact, every living thing, and so-called inanimate things also, are trees of life, with their roots above in the spiritual realms, with their trunks passing through the intermediate spheres, and their branches manifesting in the physical realms.

Ātman (Sanskrit) The root of *ātman* is hardly known; its origin is uncertain, but the general meaning is that of "self." The highest part of man — self, pure consciousness per se. The essential and radical power or faculty in man which gives to him, and indeed to every other entity or thing, its knowledge or sentient consciousness of selfhood. This is not the ego.

This principle (ātman) is a universal one; but during incarnations its lowest parts take on attributes, because it is linked with the buddhi, as the buddhi is linked with the manas, as the manas is linked to the kāma, and so on down the scale.

Ātman is also sometimes used of the universal self or spirit which is called in the Sanskrit writings Brahman (neuter), and the Brahman or universal spirit is also called the paramātman.

Man is rooted in the kosmos surrounding him by three principles, which can hardly be said to be *above* the first or ātman, but are, so to say, that same ātman's highest and most glorious parts.

The inmost link with the Unutterable was called in ancient India by the term "self," which has often been mistranslated "soul." The Sanskrit word is ātman and applies, in psychology, to the human entity. The upper end of the link, so to speak, was called paramātman, or the "self beyond," i.e., the permanent SELF — words which describe neatly and clearly to those who have studied this wonderful philosophy, somewhat of the nature and essence of the being which man is, and the source from which, in beginningless and endless duration, he sprang. Child of earth and child of heaven, he contains both in himself.

We say that the ātman is universal, and so it is. It is the universal selfhood, that feeling or consciousness of selfhood which is the same in every human being, and even in all the inferior beings of the hierarchy, even in those of the beast kingdom under us, and dimly perceptible in the plant world, and which is latent even in the minerals. This is the pure cognition, the abstract idea, of self. It differs not at all throughout the hierarchy, except in degree of self-recognition. Though universal, it belongs (so far as we are concerned in our present stage of evolution) to the fourth kosmic plane, though it is our seventh principle counting upwards.

Atom This word comes to us from the ancient Greek philosophers Democritus, Leucippus, and Epicurus, and the hundreds of great men who followed their lead in this respect and who were therefore also atomists — such, for instance, as the two Latin poets Ennius and Lucretius. This school taught that atoms were the foundation-bricks of the universe, for *atom* in the original etymological sense of the word means something that cannot be cut or divided, and therefore as being equivalent to particles of what theosophists call homogeneous substance. But modern scientists do not use the word atom in that sense any longer. Some time ago the orthodox scientific doctrine concerning the atom was basically that enunciated by Dalton, to the general effect that physical atoms were hard little particles of matter, ultimate particles of matter, and therefore indivisible and indestructible.

But modern science [1933] has a totally new view of the physical atom, for it knows now that the atom is not such, but is composite, builded of particles still more minute, called electrons or charges of negative electricity, and of other particles called protons or charges of positive electricity, which protons are supposed to form the nucleus or core of the atomic structure. A frequent picture of atomic structure is that of an atomic solar system, the protons being the atomic sun and the electrons being its planets, the latter in extremely rapid revolution around the central sun. This conception is purely theosophical in idea, and adumbrates what occultism teaches, though occultism goes much farther than does modern science.

One of the fundamental postulates of the teachings of theosophy is that the ultimates of nature are atoms on the material side and monads on the energy side. These two are respectively material and spiritual primates or ultimates, the spiritual ones or monads being indivisibles, and the atoms being divisibles — things that can be divided into composite parts.

It becomes obvious from what precedes that the philosophical idea which formed the core of the teaching of the ancient initiated atomists was that their atoms or "indivisibles" are pretty close to what theosophical occultism calls monads; and this is what Democritus and Leucippus and others of their school had in mind.

These monads, as is obvious, are therefore divine-spiritual life-atoms, and are actually beings living and evolving on their own planes. Rays from them are the highest parts of the constitution of beings in the material realms.

Aum *See* Om

Aupapāduka (Sanskrit) A compound term meaning "self-produced," "spontaneously generated." It is a term applied in Buddhism to a class of celestial beings called dhyāni-buddhas; and because these dhyāni-buddhas are conceived of as issuing forth from the bosom of Ādi-buddhi or the kosmic mahat without intermediary agency, are they mystically said to be, as H. P. Blavatsky puts it, "parentless" or "self-existing," i.e., born without any parents or progenitors. They are therefore the originants or root from which the hierarchy of buddhas of various grades flows forth in mystical procession or emanation or evolution.

There are variants of this word in Sanskrit literature, but they all have the same meaning. The term aupapāduka is actually a key word, opening a doctrine which is extremely difficult to set forth; but the doctrine itself is inexpressibly sublime. Indeed, not only are there aupapāduka divinities of the solar system, but also of every organic entity, because the core of the core of any organic entity is such an aupapāduka divinity. It is, in fact, a very mystical way of stating the doctrine of the "inner god" (q.v.).

[Note: Later research shows that *anupapādaka*, as found in Monier-Williams' *Sanskrit-English Dictionary*, is a misreading of *aupapāduka*. Cf. Franklin Edgerton, *Buddhist Hybrid Sanskrit Grammar and Dictionary*, Yale University Press, New Haven, 1953, 2:162. — Publisher]

Aura An extremely subtle and therefore invisible essence or fluid that emanates from and surrounds not only human beings and beasts, but as a matter of fact plants and minerals also. It is one of the aspects of the auric egg (q.v.) and therefore the human aura partakes of all the qualities that the human constitution contains. It is at once magneto-mental and electrovital, suffused with the energies of mind and spirit — the quality in each case coming from an organ or center of the human constitution whence it flows. It is the source of the sympathies and antipathies that we are conscious of. Under the control of the human will it can be both life-giving and healing, or death-dealing; and when the human will is passive the aura has an action of its own which is automatic and follows the laws of character and latent impulses of the being from whom it emanates. Sensitives have frequently described it in more or less vague terms as a light flowing from the eyes or the heart or the tips of the fingers or from other parts of the body. Sometimes this fluid, instead of being colorless light, manifests itself by flashing and scintillating changes of color — the color or colors in each case depending not only upon the varying moods of the human individual, but also possessing a background equivalent to the character or nature of the individual. Animals are extremely sensitive to auras, and some beasts even descry the human being surrounded with the aura as with a cloud or veil. In fact, everything has its aura surrounding it with a light or play of color, and especially is this the case with so-called animated beings.

The essential nature of the aura usually seen is astral and electrovital. The magnificent phenomena of radiation that astronomers can discern at times of eclipse, long streamers with rosy and other colored light flashing forth from the body of the sun, are not flames nor anything of the sort, but are simply the electrovital aura of the solar body — a manifestation of solar vitality, for the sun in occultism is a living being, as indeed everything else is.

Auric Egg A term which appertains solely to the more recondite teachings of occultism, of the esoteric philosophy. Little can be said here about it except to state that it is the source of the human aura as well as of everything else that the human septenary constitution contains. It is usually of an oviform or egg-shaped appearance, whence its name. It ranges from the divine to the astral-physical, and is the seat of all the monadic, spiritual, intellectual, mental, passional, and vital energies and faculties of the human septiform constitution. In its essence it is eternal, and endures throughout the pralayas as well as during the manvantaras, but necessarily in greatly varying fashion in these two great periods of kosmic life.

Avalokiteśvara (Sanskrit) A compound word: *avalokita*, "perceived," "seen"; *Īśvara*, "lord"; hence "the Lord who is perceived or cognized," i.e., the spiritual entity, whether in the kosmos or in the human being, whose influence is perceived and felt; the higher self. This is a term commonly employed in Buddhism, and concerning which a number of intricate and not easily understood teachings exist. The esoteric or occult interpretation, however, sees in Avalokiteśvara what Occidental philosophy calls the Third Logos, both celestial and human. In the solar system it is the Third Logos thereof; and in the human being it is the higher self, a direct and active ray of the divine monad. Technically Avalokiteśvara is the dhyāni-bodhisattva of Amitābha-Buddha — Amitābha-Buddha is the kosmic divine monad of which the dhyāni-bodhisattva is the individualized spiritual ray, and of this latter again the mānushya-buddha or human buddha is a ray or offspring.

Avatāra (Sanskrit) The noun-form derived from a compound of two words: *ava*, prepositional prefix meaning "down," and *tṛī*, verb-root meaning to "cross over," to "pass"; thus, *ava-tṛī* — to "pass down," or to "descend." Hence the word signifies the passing down of a celestial energy or of an individualized complex of celestial energies, which is equivalent to saying a celestial being, in order to overshadow and illuminate some human being — but a human being who, at the time of such connection of "heaven with earth," of divinity with matter, possesses no *karmically* intermediate or connecting link between the overshadowing entity and the physical body: in other words, no human soul *karmically* destined to be the inner master of the body thus born.

The intermediate link necessary, so that the human being-to-be may have the human intermediate or psychological apparatus fit to express the invisible splendor of this celestial descent, is supplied by the deliberate and voluntary entrance into the unborn child — and coincidently with the overshadowing of the celestial power — of the psychological or intermediate principle of one of the Greater Ones, who thus "completes" what is to be the pure and lofty human channel through which the "descending" divinity may manifest, this divinity finding in this high psychological principle a sufficiently evolved link enabling it to express itself in human form upon earth.

Hence an avatāra is one who has a combination of three elements in his being: an inspiring divinity; a highly evolved intermediate nature or soul, which is loaned to him and is the channel of that inspiring divinity; and a pure, clean, physical body.

Avīchi (Sanskrit) A word, the general meaning of which is "waveless," having no waves or movement, suggesting the stagnation of life and being in immobility; it also means "without happiness" or "without repose." A generalized term for places of evil realizations, but not of punishment in the Christian sense; where the will for evil, and the unsatisfied evil longings for pure selfishness, find their chance for expansion — and final extinction of the entity itself. Avīchi has many degrees or grades. Nature has all things in her; if she has heavens where good and true men find rest and peace and bliss, so has she other spheres and states where gravitate those who must find an outlet for the evil passions burning within. They, at the end of their avīchi, go to pieces and are ground over and over, and vanish away finally like a shadow before the sunlight in the air — ground over in nature's laboratory. (*See also* EIGHTH SPHERE)

Avidyā (Sanskrit) A compound word: *a*, "not"; *vidyā*, "knowledge"; hence nonknowledge, ignorance — perhaps a better translation would be nescience — ignorance or rather lack of knowledge of reality, produced by illusion or māyā (q.v.).

— B —

Bhakti Yoga (Sanskrit) A word derived from the verbal root *bhaj*. In connection with yoga and as being one of the recognized forms of it, the general signification of bhakti yoga is devotion, affectionate attachment. (*See also* YOGA)

Bhūta(s) (Sanskrit) The past participle of the verb-root *bhū*, meaning "to be," or "to become"; hence *bhūtas* literally means "has beens" — entities that have lived and passed on. The bhūtas are "shells" from which all that is spiritual and intellectual has fled: all that was the real entity has fled from this shell, and naught is left but a decaying astral corpse. The bhūtas are the spooks, ghosts, simulacra, reliquiae, of dead men; in other words, the astral dregs and remnants of human beings. They are the "shades" of the ancients, the pale and ghostly phantoms living in the astral world, or the astral copies of the men that were; and the distinction between the bhūta and the kāma-rūpa (q.v.) is very slight.

Bereft of all that pertains to the real entity, the genuine man, the bhūta is as much a corpse in the astral realms as is the decaying physical body left behind at physical death; and consequently, astral or psychical intercourse of any kind with these shells is productive only of evil. The bhūtas, although belonging in the astral world, are magnetically attracted to physical localities similar in type to the remnants of impulses still inhering in them. The bhūta of a drunkard is attracted to wine cellars and taverns; the bhūta of one who has lived a lewd life is attracted to localities sympathetic to it; the thin and tenuous bhūta of a good man is similarly attracted to less obnoxious and evil places. All over the ancient world and throughout most of even the modern world these eidola or "images" of dead men have been feared and dreaded, and relations of any kind with them have been consistently and universally avoided. (*See also* Eidolon)

Bīja (sometimes **Vīja**) (Sanskrit) This word signifies "seed" or "life-germ," whether of animals or of plants. But esoterically its signification is far wider and incomparably more abstruse, and therefore difficult to understand without proper study. The term is used in esotericism to designate the original or causal source and vāhana or "vehicle" of the mystic impulse or urge of life, or of lives, to express itself or themselves when the time for such self-expression arrives after a pralaya, or after an obscuration, or again, indeed, during manvantara. Whether it be a kosmos or universe, or the reappearance of god, deva, man, animal, plant, mineral, or elemental, the seed or life-germ from and out of which any one of these arises is technically called bīja, and the reference here is almost as much to the life-germ or vehicle itself as it is to the self-urge for manifestation working through the seed or life-germ. Mystically and psychologically, the appearance of an avatāra, for instance, is due to an impulse arising in Mahā-Śiva, or in Mahā-Vishṇu (according to circumstances), to manifest a portion of the divine essence, in either case, when the appropriate world period arrives for the appearance of an avatāra. Or again, when from the chela is born the initiate during the dread trials of initiation, the newly-arisen Master is said to have been born from the mystic bīja or seed within his own being. The doctrine connected with this word bīja in its occult and esoteric aspects is far too profound to receive more than a cursory and superficial treatment.

Black Magicians *See* BROTHERS OF THE SHADOW

Bodhi (Sanskrit) This word comes from the root *budh,* meaning "to awaken." It is the state when man has so emptied his mind that it is filled only with the self itself, with the selfless selfhood of the eternal. Then he realizes the ineffable visions of reality, of pure truth. The man who reaches this state is called a buddha, and the organ in and by which it is manifested, is termed buddhi (q.v.).

Bodhisattva (Sanskrit) A compound word: literally "he whose essence (sattva) has become intelligence (bodhi)." As explained exoterically, a bodhisattva means one who in another incarnation or in a few more incarnations will become a buddha. A bodhisattva from the standpoint of the occult teachings is more than that. When a man, a human being, has reached the state where his ego becomes conscious, fully so, of its inner divinity, becomes clothed with the buddhic ray — where, so to say, the personal man has put on the garments of inner immortality in actuality, on this earth, here and now — that man is a bodhisattva. His higher principles have nearly reached nirvāṇa. When they do so finally, such a man is a buddha, a human buddha, a mānushya-buddha. Obviously, if such a bodhisattva were to reincarnate, in the next incarnation or in a very few future incarnations thereafter, he would be a mānushya-buddha. A buddha, in the esoteric teaching, is one whose higher principles can learn nothing more. They have reached nirvāṇa and remain there; but the spiritually awakened personal man, the bodhisattva, the person made semi-divine to use popular language, instead of choosing his reward in the nirvāṇa of a less degree, remains on earth out of pity and compassion for inferior beings, and becomes what is called a nirmāṇakāya (q.v.). In a very mystical part of the esoteric philosophy, a bodhisattva is the representative on earth of a dhyāni-buddha or celestial buddha — in other words, one who has become an incarnation or expression of his own divine monad.

Brahmā (Sanskrit) A word of which the root, *bṛih*, means "expansion." It stands for the spiritual energy-consciousness side of our solar universe, i.e., our solar system, and the Egg of Brahmā is that solar system.

A Day of Brahmā or a mahā-manvantara is composed of seven rounds, a period of 4,320,000,000 terrestrial years; this period is also called a kalpa. A Night of Brahmā, the planetary rest period, which is also called the parinirvāṇic period, is of equal length.

Seven Days of Brahmā make one solar kalpa; or, in other words, seven planetary cycles, each cycle consisting of seven rounds (or seven planetary manvantaras), form one solar manvantara.

One Year of Brahmā consists of 360 Divine Days, each day being the duration of a planet's life, i.e., of a planetary chain of seven globes. The Life of Brahmā (or the life of the universal system) consists of one hundred Divine Years, i.e., 4,320,000,000 years times 36,000 x 2.

The Life of Brahmā is half ended: that is, fifty of his years are gone — a period of 155,520,000,000,000 of our years have passed away since our solar system, with its sun, first began its manvantaric course. There remain, therefore, fifty more such Years of Brahmā before the system sinks into rest or pralaya. As only half of the evolutionary journey is accomplished, we are, therefore, at the bottom of the kosmic cycle, i.e., on the lowest plane.

Brahman (Sanskrit) A word of which the root, *bṛih*, means "expansion." It is that part of the celestial being which first initiates manifestation through the various Brahmās, the expansion of the one into the many. It is what is called the unmanifest Logos. It may also be called the impersonal and uncognizable principle of the universe, and must be sharply distinguished from the masculine Brahmā of which there are many in a universe.

Note: In early theosophical literature, as well as in translations of the Hindu writings, Brahman is sometimes spelled Brahma or even Brahm; but this should not be confused with Brahmā. (*See also* PARABRAHMAN, BRAHMĀ)

Brāhmaṇa (Sanskrit) A word having several meanings in Hindu sacred literature. Brāhmaṇa is both noun and adjective, as noun signifying a member of the first of the four Vedic classes, and as adjective signifying what belongs to a Brāhmaṇa or what is Brahmanical. Secondly, it signifies one of the portions of the Vedic literature, containing rules for the proper usage of the mantras or hymns at sacrifices, explanations in detail of what these sacrifices are, illustrated by legends and old stories.

Another adjective with closely similar meaning is Brāhma. An old-fashioned English way of spelling Brāhmaṇa is Brahmin.

Brotherhood *See* UNIVERSAL BROTHERHOOD

Brother(s) of the Shadow A term given in occultism and especially in modern esotericism to individuals, whether men or women, who follow the path of the shadows, the left-hand path. The term "shadow" is a technical expression and signifies more than appears on the surface: i.e., the expression is not to be understood of individuals who live in actual physical obscurity or actual physical shadows, which literalism would be simply absurd; but applies to those who follow the path of matter, which from time immemorial in the esoteric schools in both Orient and Occident has frequently been called shadow or shadows. The term originally arose, without doubt, in the philosophical conception of the word māyā (q.v.), for in early Oriental esotericism māyā, and more especially mahā-māyā, was a term applied in one of its many philosophical meanings to that which was contrary to and, indeed, in one sense a reflection of, light. Just as spirit may be considered to be pure energy, and matter, although essentially crystallized spirit, may be looked upon as the shadow world or vehicular world in which the energy or spirit or pure light works, just so is māyā, as the garment or expression or śakti of the divine energy, the vehicle or shadow of the divine side of nature, in other words its negative or nether pole, as light is the upper or positive pole.

The Brothers of the Shadow are therefore those who, being essentially of the nature of matter, instinctively choose and follow the path along which they are most strongly drawn, that is, the path of matter or of the shadows. When it is recollected that matter is but a generalizing term, and that what this term comprises actually includes an almost infinite number of degrees of increasing ethereality from the grossest physical substance, or absolute matter, up to the most ethereal or spiritualized substance, we immediately see the subtle logic of this technical term — shadows or, more fully, the Path of the Shadows, hence the Brothers of the Shadow.

They are the so-called black magicians of the Occident, and stand in sharp and notable contrast with the white magicians or the Sons of Light who follow the pathway of self-renunciation, self-sacrifice, self-conquest, perfect self-control, and an expansion of the heart and mind and consciousness in love and service for all that lives. (*See also* RIGHT-HAND PATH)

The existence and aims of the Brothers of the Shadow are essentially selfish. It is commonly, but erroneously, supposed that the Brothers of the Shadow are men and women always of unpleasant or displeasing personal appearance, and no greater error than this could possibly be made. Multitudes of human beings are unconsciously treading the path of the shadows and, in comparison with these multitudes, it is relatively only a few who self-consciously lead and guide with subtle and nefast intelligence this army of unsuspecting victims of māyā. The Brothers of the Shadow are often highly intellectual men and women, frequently individuals with apparent great personal charm, and to the ordinary observer, judging from their conversation and daily works, are fully as well able to "quote scripture" as are the Angels of Light!

Buddha (Sanskrit) The past participle of the root *budh*, meaning "to perceive," "to become cognizant of," also "to awaken," and "to recover consciousness." It signifies one who is spiritually awakened, no longer living "the living death" of ordinary men, but awakened to the spiritual influence from within or from "above." When man has awakened from the living death in which ordinary mortals live, when he has cast off the toils of both mind and flesh and, to use the old Christian term, has put on the garments of eternity, then he has *awakened*, he is a buddha. He has become one with — not "absorbed" as is constantly translated but has *become one with* — the Self of selves, with the paramātman, the Supreme Self. (*See also* BODHI, BUDDHI)

A buddha in the esoteric teaching is one whose higher principles can learn nothing more in this manvantara; they have reached nirvāṇa and remain there. This does not mean, however, that the lower centers of consciousness of a buddha are in nirvāṇa, for the contrary is true; and it is this fact that enables a Buddha of Compassion to remain in the lower realms of being as mankind's supreme guide and instructor, living usually as a nirm̃aṇakāya.

Buddha(s) of Compassion One who, having won all, gained all — gained the right to kosmic peace and bliss — renounces it so that he may return as a Son of Light in order to help humanity, and indeed all that is.

The Buddhas of Compassion are the noblest flowers of the human race. They are men who have raised themselves from humanity into quasi-divinity; and this is done by letting the light imprisoned within, the light of the inner god, pour forth and manifest itself through the humanity of the man, through the human soul of the man. Through sacrifice and abandoning of all that is mean and wrong, ignoble and paltry and selfish; through opening up the inner nature so that the god within may shine forth; in other words, through self-directed evolution, they have raised themselves from mere manhood into becoming god-men, man-gods — human divinities.

They are called Buddhas of Compassion because they feel their unity with all that is, and therefore feel intimate magnetic sympathy with all that is, and this is more and more the case as they evolve, until finally their consciousness blends with that of the universe and lives eternally and immortally, because it is at one with the universe. "The dewdrop slips into the shining sea" — its origin.

Feeling the urge of almighty love in their hearts, the Buddhas of Compassion advance forever steadily towards still greater heights of spiritual achievement; and the reason is that they have become the vehicles of universal love and universal wisdom. As impersonal love is universal, their whole nature expands consequently with the universal powers that are working through them. The Buddhas of Compassion, existing in their various degrees of evolution, form a sublime hierarchy extending from the Silent Watcher on our planet downwards through these various degrees unto themselves, and even beyond themselves to their chelas or disciples. Spiritually and mystically they contrast strongly with what Asiatic occultism, through the medium of Buddhism, has called the Pratyeka Buddhas (q.v.).

Buddhi (Sanskrit) Buddhi comes from a Sanskrit root *budh*, commonly translated "to enlighten," but a better translation is "to perceive," "to cognize," "to recover consciousness," hence "to awaken," and therefore "to understand." The second counting downwards, or the sixth counting upwards, of the seven principles of man. Buddhi is the principle or organ in man which gives to him spiritual consciousness, and is the vehicle of the most high part of man — the ātman — the faculty which manifests as understanding, judgment, discrimination, an inseparable veil or garment of the ātman.

From another point of view, buddhi may truly be said to be both the seed and the fruit of manas.

Man's ordinary consciousness in life in his present stage of evolution is almost wholly in the lower or intermediate duad (manas-kāma) of his constitution; when he raises his consciousness through personal effort to become permanently one with the higher duad (ātma-buddhi), he becomes a mahātma, a master. At the death of the human being, this higher duad carries away with it all the spiritual essence, all the spiritual and intellectual aroma, of the lower or intermediate duad. Mahā-buddhi is one of the names given to the kosmic principle mahat. (*See also* ALAYA)

Buddhism The teachings of Gautama the Buddha. Buddhism today is divided into two branches, the Northern and the Southern. The Southern still retains the teachings of the "Buddha's brain," the "eye doctrine," that is to say his outer philosophy for the general world, sometimes inadequately called the doctrine of forms and ceremonies. The Northern still retains his "heart doctrine" — that which is hid, the inner life, the heart-blood, of the religion: the doctrine of the inner heart of the teaching.

The religious philosophy of the Buddha-Śākyamuni is incomparably nearer to the ancient wisdom, the esoteric philosophy of the archaic ages, than is Christianity. Its main fault today is that teachers later than the Buddha himself carried its doctrines too far along merely formal or exoteric lines; yet, with all that, to this day it remains the purest and holiest of the exoteric religions on earth, and its teachings even exoterically are true — once they are properly understood. They need but the esoteric key in interpretation of them. As a matter of fact, the same may be said of all the great ancient world religions. Christianity, Brahmanism, Taoism, and others all have the same esoteric wisdom behind the outward veil of the exoteric formal faith.

— C —

Cakra *See* Chakra

Causal Body For a proper explanation of the doctrine connected with this term the student is referred to kāraṇa-śarīra and kāraṇopādhi as defined in this volume. Technically speaking, causal body is a misnomer, for, in fact, the element of man's constitution here referred to and, *mutatis mutandis,* when reference is made to beings above and below man, is no body at all, properly speaking, but rather what one might call a soul, although strenuous objection could very logically be taken to the use of this word soul because of the many and often contradictory meanings that common usage has given to it.

Furthermore, the expression "causal body" refers to two different things. The meaning, therefore, is dual — a statement which will be explained under kāraṇopādhi. It may be stated here, however, that the two meanings have reference, the first to a lower part of man's septenary constitution, and the second to a higher part, both parts acting as causes, or instrumental causes, in producing reappearances, or new manifestations, of a reimbodying monad or entity.

Cela *See* Chela

Chain *See* Planetary Chain

Chakra (*Cakra*, Sanskrit) A word signifying in general a "wheel," and from this simple original meaning there were often taken for occult and esoteric purposes a great many subordinate, very interesting, and in some cases highly mystical and profound derivatives. Chakra also means a cycle, a period of duration, in which the wheel of time turns once. It also means the horizon, as being circular or of a wheel-form. It likewise means certain centers or prāṇic spherical loci of the body in which are supposed to collect streams of prāṇic energy of differing qualities, or prāṇic energies of different kinds. These physiological chakras, which are actually connected with the prāṇic circulations and ganglia of the auric egg, and therefore function in the physical body through the intermediary of the liṅga-śarīra or astral model-body, are located in different parts of the physical frame, reaching from the parts about the top of the skull to the parts about the pubis. It would be highly improper, having at heart the best interests of humanity, to give the occult or esoteric teaching concerning the exact location, functions, and means of controlling the physiological chakras of the human body; for it is a foregone conclusion that were this mystical knowledge broadcast, it would be sadly misused, leading not only in many cases to death or insanity, but to the violation of every moral instinct. Alone the high initiates, who as a matter of fact have risen above the need of employing the physiological chakras, can use them at will, and for holy purposes — which in fact is something that they rarely, if indeed they ever do.

Chaos (Greek) A word usually thought to mean a sort of helter-skelter treasury of original principles and seeds of beings. Well, so it verily is, in one profound sense; but it is most decidedly and emphatically not helter-skelter. It is properly the kosmic storehouse of all the latent or resting seeds of beings and things from former manvantaras. Of course it is this, simply because it contains everything. It means space, not the highest mystical or actual space, not the parabrahma-mūlaprakṛiti, the Boundless — not that. But the space of any particular hierarchy descending into manifestation, what space for it is at that particular period of its beginning of development. The directive principles in chaos are the gods when they awaken from their pralayic sleep. Chaos in one sense may very truly be called the condition of the space of a solar system or even of a planetary chain during its pralaya (q.v.). When awakening to planetary action begins, chaos *pari passu* ceases.

Chela (*Cela*) An old Indian term. In archaic times more frequently spelled and pronounced cheṭa or cheḍa. The meaning is "servant," a personal disciple attached to the service of a teacher from whom he receives instruction. The idea is closely similar to the Anglo-Saxon term *leorning-cneht*, meaning "learning servant," a name given in Anglo-Saxon translations of the Christian New Testament to the disciples of Jesus, his "chelas." It is, therefore, a word used in old mystical scriptures for a disciple, a pupil, a learner or hearer. The relationship of teacher and disciple is infinitely more sacred even than that of parent and child; because, while the parents give the body to the incoming soul, the teacher brings forth that soul itself and teaches it to be and therefore to see, teaches it to know and to *become* what it is in its inmost being — that is, a divine thing.

The chela life or chela path is a beautiful one, full of joy to its very end, but also it calls forth and needs everything noble and high in the learner or disciple; for the powers or faculties of the higher self must be brought into activity in order to attain and to hold those summits of intellectual and spiritual grandeur where the Masters themselves live. For that, masterhood, is the end of discipleship — not, however, that this ideal should be set before us merely as an end to attain to as something of benefit for one's own self, because that very thought is a selfish one and therefore a stumbling in the path. It is for the individual's benefit, of course; yet the true idea is that everything and every faculty that is in the soul shall be brought out in the service of all humanity, for this is the royal road, the great royal thoroughfare, of self-conquest. The more mystical meanings attached to this term chela can be given only to those who have irrevocably pledged themselves to the esoteric life.

Chhāyā (*Chāyā,* Sanskrit) Literally a "shade," "simulacrum," or "copy." In the esoteric philosophy, the word signifies the astral image of a person, and with this idea are bound up some of the most intricate and recondite teachings of human evolution. *The Secret Doctrine* of H. P. Blavatsky contains many invaluable hints as to the part played by the chhāyās of the pitṛis in human development.

It is a word also which is applied with similar meaning to kosmical matters, for the esoteric student should never forget the ancient maxim of Hermes: "What is above is the same as what is below; what is below is the same as what is above."

Briefly, then, and so far as human evolution is concerned, the chhāyā may be called the astral body (q.v.) or image.

Chit *See* SAT

Christos (Greek) Christos or "Christ" is a word literally signifying one who has been "anointed." This is a direct reference, a direct allusion, to what happened during the celebration of the ancient Mysteries. Unction or anointing was one of the acts performed during the working of the rites of those ancient Mysteries in the countries surrounding the Mediterranean Sea. The Hebrew word for an anointed one is *māshīahh* — "messiah" is a common way of misspelling the Hebrew word — meaning exactly the same thing as the Greek word Christos.

Each human being is an incarnation, an imbodiment, of a ray of his own inner god — the divinity living in the core of the core of each one. The modern Christians of a mystical bent of mind call it the Christ Immanent, the immanent Christos, and they are right as far as they go, but they do not carry the thought far enough. Mystically speaking, the Christos is the deathless individuality; and when the striving personal ego becomes united permanently with this stainless individuality, the resultant union is the higher ego, "the living Christ" — a Christ among men, or as the Buddhists would say, a human or mānushya-buddha.

Circulations of the Kosmos Also Circulations of the Universe. This is a term used in the ancient wisdom or esoteric philosophy to signify the network, marvelously intricate and builded of the channels or canals or paths or roads followed by peregrinating or migrating entities as these latter pass from sphere to sphere or from realm to realm or from plane to plane. The pilgrim monads, however far advanced or however little advanced in their evolution, inevitably and ineluctably follow these circulations. They can do nothing else, for they are simply the spiritual, psychomagnetic, astral, and physical pathways along which the forces of the universe flow; and consequently, all entities whatsoever being indeed imbodiments of forces must of necessity follow the same routes or pathways that the abstract forces themselves use.

These circulations of the kosmos are a veritable network between planet and planet, and planet and sun, and between sun and sun, and between sun and universe, and between universe and universe. Furthermore, the circulations of the kosmos are not restricted to the material or astral spheres, but are of the very fabric and structure of the entire universal kosmos, inner as well as outer. It is one of the most mystical and suggestive doctrines of theosophy.

Clairaudience In its largest sense the word means simply "clear-hearing." True clairaudience is a spiritual faculty, the faculty of the inner spiritual ear, of which the psychical clairaudience is but a distorted and therefore deceptive reflection; neither is it hearing with the physical ear, so imperfect and undeveloped a sensory organ as the latter is. The power to hear with the inner ear enables you to hear anything you will, and at whatever distance, whether on Mars, or on the Sun, or on the Moon, or on Jupiter, or perhaps even on some distant star, or easily anywhere on Earth. Having this spiritual clairaudience, you can hear the grass grow, and that hearing will be to you like a symphonic musical poem. You can hear the celestial orbs singing their songs as they advance along their orbits through space, because everything that is, is in movement, producing sound, simple or composite as the case may be. Thus in very truth every tiny atom sings its own note, and every composite entity, therefore, is an imbodied musical poem, a musical symphony. (*See also* Music of the Spheres)

Clairvoyance In its largest sense the word simply means "clear-seeing," insight behind the veils, inner visioning. Genuine clairvoyance is a spiritual faculty and is the ability to see and to see aright; and in seeing to know that your seeing is truth. This is no psychical faculty. The clairvoyance commonly called the psychical clairvoyance is very deceptive, because it is a mere moonlight reflection so to speak, and this moonlight reflection is uncertain, deceiving, and illusory. Genuine spiritual clairvoyance, of which the psychical clairvoyance so called is but a feeble ray, will enable one to see what passes at immense distances. You can sit in your armchair and see, with eyes closed, all that you care to see, however far away. This can be done not only in this exterior world, but one can penetrate into the interior and invisible worlds with this spiritual vision, and thus know what is going on in the worlds spiritual and ethereal. This vision is not physical vision, nor that which, on the astral plane, manifests itself as psychical clairvoyance; but true vision is spiritual clairvoyance — seeing through the inner spiritual eye.

Consciousness In all its forms and protean manifestations, consciousness is spirit-matter — force and matter, or spirit and substance, are one — hence consciousness is the finest and loftiest form of energy, is the root of all things, and is coextensive with kosmic space. It is, therefore, the foundation and the essence of gods, of monads, and of atoms — the three generalized degrees, kosmically speaking, of the universe. A natural corollary from this is that the universe therefore is imbodied consciousness, or much more correctly we should call it a quasi-infinite aggregate of imbodied consciousnesses.

Cosmos Whenever a theosophist speaks of the cosmos or the universe, he by no means refers only to the physical sphere or world or cross section of the boundless All in which we humans live, but more particularly to the invisible worlds and planes and spheres inhabited by their countless hosts of vitalized or animate beings. In order to avoid redundancy of words and often confusing repetitions in the midst of an explanation dealing with other matters, since H. P. Blavatsky's time it has been customary among careful theosophical writers to draw a distinction of fact between cosmos and kosmos. The solar universe or solar system is frequently referred to as cosmos or solar cosmos; and the galactic universe or our own home-universe it has been customary to refer to as the kosmos. This distinction, however, does not always hold, because sometimes in dealing with abstract questions where the application of the thought can be indifferently made either to the galactic or to the solar universe, the two forms of spelling may be used interchangeably. (*See also* KOSMOS, KOSMIC LIFE)

Cycles or **Law of Cycles** An exceedingly interesting branch of theosophical study, and one dealing with a fact which is so obviously manifest in the worlds surrounding us that its existence can hardly be denied, except by the willfully blind, is what may be called the law of cycles, or nature's repetitive operations.

We find nature repeating herself everywhere, although such repetition of course is not merely a running in the same old ruts on each recurrence of the cyclic activity; for each recurrence is of course the expression of a modification, more or less great, of what has preceded. Day succeeds night, winter succeeds summer, the planets circulate around the suns in regular and periodical courses; and these are but familiar examples of cyclical activity.

Cycles in nature show the time periods of periodic recurrence along and in which any evolving entity or thing expresses the energies and powers which are itself, so that cycles and evolution are like the two sides of a coin: the one shows the time periods or cycles, and the other side manifests the energic or substantial qualities appearing in manifestation according to these cyclical time-periods; but back of this apparently double but actually single process always lie profound karmic causes.

— D —

Daivīprakṛiti (Sanskrit) A compound signifying "divine" or "original evolver," or "original source," of the universe or of any self-contained or hierarchical portion of such universe, such as a solar system. Briefly, therefore, daivīprakṛiti may be called "divine matter," matter here being used in its original sense of "divine *mother-evolver*" or "divine *original substance*."

Now, as original substance manifests itself in the kosmic spaces as primordial kosmic light — light in occult esoteric theosophical philosophy being a form of original matter or substance — many mystics have referred to daivīprakṛiti under the phrase "the Light of the Logos." Daivīprakṛiti is, in fact, the first veil or sheath or ethereal body surrounding the Logos, as pradhāna or prakṛiti surrounds Purusha or Brahman in the Sānkhya philosophy, and as, on a scale incomparably more vast, mūlaprakṛiti surrounds parabrahman. As daivīprakṛiti, therefore, is elemental matter, or matter in its sixth and seventh stages counting from physical matter upwards or, what comes to the same thing, matter in its first and second stages of its evolution from above, we may accurately enough speak of those filmy ethereal wisps of light seen in the midnight skies as a physical manifestation of daivīprakṛiti, because when they are not actually resolvable nebulae, they are worlds, or rather systems of worlds, in the making.

When daivīprakṛiti has reached a certain state or condition of evolutionary manifestation, we may properly speak of it under the term fohat (q.v.). Fohat, in H. P. Blavatsky's words, is

> The essence of cosmic electricity. An occult Tibetan term for *Daivī-*

> *prakṛiti,* primordial light: and in the universe of manifestation the ever-present electrical energy and ceaseless destructive and formative power. Esoterically, it is the same, Fohat being the universal propelling Vital Force, at once the propeller and the resultant.
>
> — *Theosophical Glossary,* p. 121

All this is extremely well put, but it must be remembered that although fohat is the energizing power working in and upon manifested daivīprakṛiti, or primordial substance, as the rider rides the steed, it is the kosmic intelligence, or kosmic monad as Pythagoras would say, working through both daivīprakṛiti and its differentiated energy called fohat, which is the guiding and controlling principle, not only in the kosmos but in every one of the subordinate elements and beings of the hosts of multitudes of them infilling the kosmos. The heart or essence of the sun is daivīprakṛiti working as itself, and also in its manifestation called fohat, but through the daivīprakṛiti and the fohatic aspect of it runs the all-permeant and directive intelligence of the solar divinity. The student should never make the mistake, however, of divorcing this guiding solar intelligence from its veils or vehicles, one of the highest of which is daivīprakṛiti-fohat.

Death Death occurs when a general break-up of the constitution of man takes place; nor is this break-up a matter of sudden occurrence, with the exceptions of course of such cases as mortal accidents or suicides. Death is always preceded, varying in each individual case, by a certain time spent in the withdrawal of the monadic individuality from an incarnation, and this withdrawal of course takes place coincidently with a decay of the seven-principle being which man is in physical incarnation. This decay precedes physical dissolution, and is a preparation of and by the consciousness-center for the forthcoming existence in the invisible realms. This withdrawal actually is a preparation for the life to come in invisible realms, and as the septenary entity on this earth so decays, it may truly be said to be approaching rebirth in the next sphere.

Death occurs, physically speaking, with the cessation of activity of the pulsating heart. There is the last beat, and this is followed by immediate, instantaneous unconsciousness, for nature is very merciful in these things. But death is not yet complete, for the brain is the last organ of the physical body really to die, and for some time after the heart has ceased beating, the brain and its memory still remain active and, although unconsciously so, the human ego for this short length of time, passes in review every event of the preceding life. This great or small panoramic picture of the past is purely automatic, so to say; yet the soul-consciousness of the reincarnating ego watches this wonderful review incident by incident, a review which includes the entire course of thought and action of the life just closed. The entity is, for the time being, entirely unconscious of everything else except this. Temporarily it lives in the past, and memory dislodges from the ākāśic record, so to speak, event after event, to the smallest detail: passes them all in review, and in regular order from the beginning to the end, and thus sees all its past life as an all-inclusive panorama of picture succeeding picture.

There are very definite ethical and psychological reasons inhering in this process, for this process forms a reconstruction of both the good and the evil done in the past life, and imprints this strongly as a record on the fabric of the spiritual memory of the passing being. Then the mortal and material portions sink into oblivion, while the reincarnating ego (q.v.) carries the best and noblest parts of these memories into the devachan (q.v.) or heaven-world of postmortem rest and recuperation. Thus comes the end called death; and unconsciousness, complete and undisturbed, succeeds, until there occurs what the ancients called the second death (q.v.).

The lower triad (prāṇa, liṅga-śarīra, sthūla-śarīra, q.v.) is now definitely cast off, and the remaining quaternary is free. The physical body of the lower triad follows the course of natural decay, and its various hosts of life-atoms proceed whither their natural attractions draw them. The liṅga-śarīra or model-body remains in the astral realms, and finally fades out. The life-atoms of the prāṇa, or electrical field, fly instantly back at the moment of physical dissolution to the natural prāṇic reservoirs of the planet.

This leaves man, therefore, no longer a heptad or septenary entity, but a quaternary consisting of the upper duad (ātma-buddhi) and the intermediate duad (manas-kāma). The second death then takes place.

Death and the adjective *dead* are mere words by which the human mind seeks to express thoughts which it gathers from a more or less consistent observation of the phenomena of the material world. Death is dissolution of a component entity or thing. The dead, therefore, are merely dissolving bodies — entities which have reached their term on this our physical plane. Dissolution is common to all things, because all physical things are composite: they are not absolute things. They are born; they grow; they reach maturity; they enjoy, as the expression runs, a certain term of life in the full bloom of their powers; then they "die." That is the ordinary way of expressing what men call death; and the corresponding adjective is *dead*, when we say that such things or entities are dead.

Do you find death per se anywhere? No. You find nothing but action; you find nothing but movement; you find nothing but change. Nothing stands still or is annihilated. What is called death itself shouts forth to us the fact of movement and change. Absolute inertia is unknown in nature or in the human mind; it does not exist.

Descending Arc (or **Shadowy Arc**) *See* Ascending Arc

Devachan [Tibetan, *bde-ba-can*, pronounced *de-wa-chen*] A translation of the Sanskrit *sukhāvatī*, the "happy place" or god-land. It is the state between earth-lives into which the human entity, the human monad, enters and there rests in bliss and repose.

When the second death (q.v.) after that of the physical body takes place — and there are many deaths, that is to say many changes of the vehicles of the ego — the higher part of the human entity withdraws into itself all that aspires towards it, and takes that "all" with it into the devachan; and the ātman, with the buddhi and with the higher part of the manas, become thereupon the spiritual monad of man. Devachan as a state applies not to the highest or heavenly or divine monad, but only to the middle principles of man, to the personal ego or the personal soul in man, overshadowed by ātma-buddhi. There are many degrees in devachan: the highest, the intermediate, and the lowest. Yet devachan is not a locality, it is a state, a state of the beings in that spiritual condition.

Devachan is the fulfilling of all the unfulfilled spiritual hopes of the past incarnation, and an efflorescence of all the spiritual and intellectual yearnings of the past incarnation which in that past incarnation have not had an opportunity for fulfillment. It is a period of unspeakable bliss and peace for the human soul, until it has finished its rest time and stage of recuperation of its own energies.

In the devachanic state, the reincarnating ego remains in the bosom of the monad (or of the monadic essence) in a state of the most perfect and utter bliss and peace, reviewing and constantly reviewing, and improving upon in its own blissful imagination, all the unfulfilled spiritual and intellectual possibilities of the life just closed that its naturally creative faculties automatically suggest to the devachanic entity.

Man here is no longer a quaternary of substance-principles (for the second death has taken place), but is now reduced to the monad with the reincarnating ego sleeping in its bosom, and is therefore a spiritual triad. (*See also* DEATH, REINCARNATING EGO)

Deva(s) (Sanskrit) A word meaning celestial being, of which there are various classes. This has been a great puzzle for most of our Occidental Orientalists. They cannot understand the distinctions that the wonderful old philosophers of the Orient make as regards the various classes of the devas. They say, in substance: "What funny contradictions there are in these teachings, which in many respects are profound and seem wonderful. Some of these devas or divine beings are said to be *less* than man; some of these writings even say that a good man is nobler than any god. And yet other parts of these teachings declare that there are gods higher even than the devas, and yet are called devas. What does this mean?"

The devas or celestial beings, one class of them, are the unself-conscious sparks of divinity, cycling down into matter in order to bring out *from within themselves* and to unfold or evolve *self*-consciousness, the svabhāva (q.v.) of divinity within. They then begin their reascent always on the luminous arc, which never ends, in a sense; and they are gods, *self*-conscious gods, *henceforth* taking a definite and divine part in the "great work," as the mystics have said, of being builders, evolvers, leaders of hierarchies. In other words, they are monads *which have become their own innermost selves,* which have passed the ring-pass-not (q.v.) separating the spiritual from the divine.

Dhāraṇā (Sanskrit) A state in the practice of yoga as taught in Hindustan when the mind or percipient intelligence is held with inflexible firmness, with fortitude of soul, and with indomitable resolution upon the object of investigation to be attained through this form of yoga practice. (*See also* Samādhi)

Dharma (Sanskrit) A noun derived from the verbal root *dhṛi.* The meaning is right religion, right philosophy, right science, and the right union of these three; hence the Law per se. It also means equity, justice, conduct, duty, and similar things. It has also a secondary meaning of an essential or characteristic quality or peculiarity; and here its significance approaches closely to that of svabhāva (q.v.). The duty of a man, for instance, is his dharma, that which is set or prescribed or natural to him to do.

Dharmakāya (Sanskrit) This is a compound of two words meaning the "continuance body," sometimes translated equally well (or ill) the "body of the Law" — both very inadequate expressions, for the difficulty in translating these extremely mystical terms is very great. A mere correct dictionary-translation often misses the esoteric meaning entirely, and just here is where Occidental scholars make such ludicrous errors at times.

The first word comes from the root *dhṛi*, meaning "to support," "to sustain," "to carry," "to bear," hence "to continue"; also human laws are the agencies supposed to carry, support, sustain, civilization; the second element, *kāya*, means "body." The noun thus formed may be rendered the "body of the Law," but this phrase does not give the idea at all. It is that spiritual body or state of a high spiritual being in which the restricted sense of soulship and egoity has vanished into a universal (hierarchical) sense, and remains only in the seed, latent — if even so much. It is pure consciousness, pure bliss, pure intelligence, freed from all personalizing thought.

In the Buddhism of Central Asia, the dharmakāya is the third and highest of the *trikāya*. The trikāya consists of (1) nirmāṇakāya, (2) sambhogakāya, and (3) dharmakāya. We may look upon these three states, all of them lofty and sublime, as being three vestures in which the consciousness of the entity clothes itself. In the dharmakāya vesture the initiate is already on the threshold of nirvāṇa (q.v.), if not indeed already in the nirvāṇic state. (*See also* NIRMĀṆAKĀYA, SAMBHOGAKĀYA)

Dhyāna (Sanskrit) A term signifying profound spiritual-intellectual contemplation with utter detachment from all objects of a sensuous and lower mental character. In Buddhism it is one of the six pāramitās of perfection. One who is adept or expert in the practice of dhyāna, which by the way is a wonderful spiritual exercise if the proper idea of it be grasped, is carried in thought entirely out of all relations with the material and merely psychological spheres of being and of consciousness, and into lofty spiritual planes. Instead of dhyāna being a subtraction from the elements of consciousness, it is rather a throwing off or casting aside of the crippling sheaths of ethereal matter which surround the consciousness, thus allowing the dhyānin, or practicer of this form of true yoga, to enter into the highest parts of his own constitution and temporarily to become at one with and, therefore, to commune with the gods. It is a temporary becoming at one with the upper triad of man considered as a septenary, in other words, with his monadic essence. Man's consciousness in this state or condition becomes purely buddhi, or rather buddhic, with the highest parts of the manas acting as upādhi or vehicle for the retention of what the consciousness therein experiences. From this term is drawn the phrase dhyāni-chohans (q.v.) or dhyāni-buddhas — words so frequently used in theosophical literature and so frequently misconceived as to their real meaning. (*See also* Samādhi)

Dhyān(i)-Chohan(s) A compound word meaning "lords of meditation" — kosmic spirits or planetary spirits. There are three classes of dhyān-chohans, each of which is divided into seven subclasses. The dhyān-chohans collectively are one division of that wondrous host of spiritual beings who are the full-blown flowers of former world periods or manvantaras. This wondrous host are the men made perfect of those former world periods; and they guide the evolution of this planet in its present manvantara. They are our own spiritual lords, leaders, and saviors. They supervise us now in our evolution here, and in our own present cyclic pilgrimage we follow the path of the general evolution outlined by them.

Man in his higher nature is an embryo dhyān-chohan, an embryo lord of meditation. It is his destiny, if he run the race successfully, to blossom forth at the end of the seventh round as a lord of meditation — a planetary spirit — when this planetary manvantaric kalpa is ended, this Day of Brahmā, which is the seven rounds, each round in seven stages.

In one most important sense the dhyān-chohans are actually our own *selves.* We were born from them. We are the monads, we are the atoms, the souls, projected, sent forth, emanated, by the dhyānīs.

Divine Soul In occultism the divine soul is the garment of the divine ego, as the divine ego is the garment or child of the divine monad. The divine monad we may call the inner god, and this would mean that the divine ego, its offspring, is the inner Buddha, or the inner Christ; and hence the divine soul is the expression of the inner Buddha or of the inner Christ in manifestation on earth as the mānushya-buddha or christ-man.

It should be stated here that of the several monads which in their combination form the entire septenary constitution of man each such monad has its own ego-child, and this latter has its own soul. It is this combination, mystic, wonderful, mysterious, which makes of man the complex entity he is, and which entitles him to the term which the occultism of the archaic ages has always given to him: the microcosm (q.v.), a reflection or copy in the small of the macrocosm (q.v.) or kosmic entity.

Dvāpara Yuga (*See* YUGA)

Dweller on the Threshold A literary invention of the English mystic and novelist Sir Bulwer Lytton, found in his romance *Zanoni.* The term has obtained wide currency and usage in theosophical circles. In occultism the word "dweller," or some exactly equivalent phrase or expression, has been known and used during long ages past. It refers to several things, but more particularly has an application to what H. P. Blavatsky calls "certain maleficent astral Doubles of defunct persons." This is exact. But there is another meaning of this phrase still more mystical and still more difficult to explain which refers to the imbodied karmic consequences or results of the man's past, haunting the thresholds which the initiant or initiate must pass before he can advance or progress into a higher degree of initiation. These dwellers, in the significance of the word just last referred to are, as it were, the imbodied quasi-human astral haunting parts of the constitution thrown off in past incarnations by the man who now has to face them and overcome them — very real and living beings, parts of the "new" man's haunting past. The initiant must face these old "selves" of himself and conquer or — fail, which failure may mean either insanity or death. They are verily ghosts of the dead men that the present man formerly was, now arising to dog his footsteps, and hence are very truly called Dwellers on the Threshold. In a specific sense they may be truly called the kāma-rūpas of the man's past incarnations arising out of the records in the astral light left there by the "old" man of the "new" man who now is.

— E —

Ego (Latin) A word meaning "I." In theosophical writings the ego is that which says "I am I" — indirect or reflected consciousness, consciousness reflected back upon itself as it were, and thus recognizing its own māyāvi existence as a "separate" entity. On this fact is based the one genuine "heresy" that occultism recognizes: the heresy of separateness.

The seat of the human ego is the intermediate duad — manas-kāma: part aspiring upwards, which is the reincarnating ego; and part attracted below, which is the ordinary or astral human ego. The consciousness is immortal in the reincarnating ego, and temporary or mortal in the lower or astral human ego.

Consider the hierarchy of the human being's constitution to grow from the immanent Self: this last is the seed of egoity on the seven (or perhaps better, six) planes of matter or manifestation. On each one of these seven planes (or six), the immanent Self or paramātman develops or evolves a sheath or garment, the upper ones spun of spirit, and the lower ones spun of "shadow" or matter. Now each such sheath or garment is a "soul"; and between the self and such a soul — any soul — is the ego.

Thus ātman is the divine monad, giving birth to the divine ego, which latter evolves forth the monadic envelope or divine soul; jīvātman, the spiritual monad, has its child which is the spiritual ego, which in turn evolves forth the spiritual soul or individual; and the combination of these three considered as a unit is buddhi; bhūtātman, the human ego — the higher human soul, including the lower buddhi and higher manas; prāṇātman, the personal ego — the lower human soul, or man. It includes manas, kāma, and prāṇa; and finally the beast ego — the vital-astral soul: kāma and prāṇa (*see* these various terms).

Eidolon (Greek; plural *eidola*) A word meaning "image" of the man that was. After death there remains in the astral world — which is on the other side of the threshold of physical life, the etheric world — the "shadow" of the man that was. The ancients called these human shadows, shades; modern children and nursemaids call them ghosts and spooks; and each such shade is but an eidolon, or astral image or pale copy of the physical man that was. This eidolon coheres for a while in the astral realms or in the superphysical ether, and its particles are magnetically held more or less coherent as long as the physical corpse is not fully dissolved into its component elements; but these eidola in a comparatively short time fade out, for they decay in a manner closely resembling the disintegration of the physical body.

Eighth Sphere or **Planet of Death** A term used in the more esoteric or inner part of the teachings about which little can be said, for over this part of the doctrine there has always been drawn a thick veil of secrecy and silence.

Frequently the term is confused with avīchi (q.v.), but this is incorrect, because the two, while closely connected, are nevertheless quite distinct. While avīchi is a state where very evil human beings "*die and are reborn without interruption,*" yet not without hope of final redemption — something which can actually take place even on our physical plane in the cases of very evil or soulless men — the Eighth Sphere represents a degree of psychomental degeneration still more advanced. As just hinted, even in avīchi there is a possibility of reinsoulment by the ray of the spiritual monad; whereas in the Eighth Sphere or Planet of Death such possibility finally vanishes, and the entity which has sunk to the Planet of Death is what is technically called in the esoteric philosophy a "lost soul." In the Eighth Sphere the lost souls are ground over and over in nature's laboratory, and are finally dissipated into their component psycho-astral elements or life-atoms. The Eighth Sphere or Planet of Death is an actual globe. It is also of course a state or condition of being; whereas the avīchi is almost exclusively a state or condition in which an entity may find itself, although obviously this entity must have position or place and therefore locality in space — on our earth or elsewhere.

Ekāgratā or **Ekāgratva** (Sanskrit) A term signifying "one-pointedness" or "absolute intentness" in the mental contemplation of an object of meditation. The perfect concentration of the percipient mind on a single point of thought, and the holding of it there.

Elemental(s) Nature-spirits or sprites. The theosophical usage, however, means beings who are beginning a course of evolutionary growth, and who thus are in the *elemental* states of their growth. It is a generalizing term for purposes of convenient expression for all beings evolutionally below the minerals. Nevertheless, the minerals themselves are expressions of one family or host or hierarchy of elemental beings of a more evolved type. The vegetable kingdom likewise manifests merely one family or host of elemental beings happening to be in the vegetable phase of their evolution on this earth. Just so likewise is it as regards the beasts. The beasts are highly evolved elemental beings, relatively speaking. Men in far distant aeons of the kosmic past were elemental beings also. We have evolved from that elemental stage into becoming men, expressing with more or less ease, mostly very feebly, the innate divine powers and faculties locked up in the core of the core of each one of us.

An elemental is a being who has entered our universe on the lowest plane or in the lowest world, degree, or step on the rising stairway of life; and this stairway of life begins in any universe at its lowest stage, and ends for that universe in its highest stage — the universal kosmic spirit. Thus the elemental passes from the elemental stage through all the realms of being as it rises along the stairway of life, passing through the human stage, becoming superhuman, quasi-divine — a quasi-god — then becoming a god. Thus did we humans first enter this present universe.

Every race of men on earth has believed in these hosts of elemental entities — some visible, like men, like the beasts, like the animate plants; and others invisible. The invisible entities have been called by various names: fairies, sprites, hobgoblins, elves, brownies, pixies, nixies, leprechauns, trolls, kobolds, goblins, banshees, fawns, devs, jinn, satyrs, and so forth. The medieval mystics taught that these elemental beings were of four general kinds: those arising in and frequenting the element of fire — salamanders; those arising in and frequenting the element air — sylphs; those arising in and frequenting the element water — undines; those arising in and frequenting the element earth — gnomes.

Elementaries "Properly, the disembodied *souls* of the depraved; these souls having at some time prior to death separated from themselves their divine spirits, and so lost their chance for immortality" (*Theosophical Glossary*, H. P. Blavatsky).

Strictly speaking, the word "elementaries" should be used as H. P. Blavatsky defines it in this quotation from her. But in modern theosophical literature the word has come to signify more particularly the phantoms or eidola (q.v.) of disembodied persons, these phantoms or eidola really being the kāma-rūpic shades, with especial application to the cases of grossly materialistic ex-humans whose evil impulses and appetites still inhering in the kāma-rūpic phantom draw these phantoms to physical spheres congenial to them. They are a real danger to psychical health and sanity, and literally haunt living human beings possessing tendencies akin to their own. They are soulless shells, but still filled with energies of a depraved and ignoble type. Their destiny of course is like that of all other pretas or bhūtas — ultimate disintegration; for the gross astral atoms composing them slowly dissolve through the years after the manner of a dissolving column of smoke or a wisp of dark cloud on a mountainside.

Esoteric Doctrine The body of mystical and sacred teachings reserved for students of high and worthy character. This body of teachings has been known and studied by highly evolved individuals in all ages. The esoteric doctrine is the common property of mankind, and it has always been thus. In all the various great religions and philosophies of the world, the student will find fundamental principles in each which, when placed side by side and critically examined, are easily discovered to be identic. Every one of such fundamental principles is in every great world religion or world philosophy; hence the aggregate of these world religions or world philosophies contains the entirety of the esoteric doctrine, but usually expressed in exoteric form.

However, no one of these world religions or world philosophies gives in clear and explicit shape or form the entirety of the body of teachings which are at its heart; some religions emphasize one or more of such fundamental principles; another religion or philosophy will emphasize others of these principles; in either case others again of the principles remaining in the background. This readily accounts for the fact that the various world religions and world philosophies vary among themselves and often, to the unreflecting mind, superficially seem to have little in common, and perhaps even to be contradictory. The cause of this is the varying manner in which each such religion or philosophy has been given to the world, the form that each took having been best for the period in which it was promulgated. Each such religion or philosophy, having its own racial sphere and period of time, represents the various human minds who have developed it or who, so to say, have translated it to the world in this or in that particular promulgation.

These manners or mannerisms of exoteric thinking we may discard if we wish; but it is the fundamental principles behind every great religion or great philosophy which in their aggregate are the universal esoteric doctrine. In this universal esoteric doctrine lies the mystery-field of each great religion or philosophy — this mystery-teaching being always reserved for the initiates. The esoteric philosophy or doctrine has been held from time immemorial in the guardianship of great men, exalted seers and sages, who from time to time promulgate it, or rather portions of it, to the world when the spiritual and intellectual need for so doing arises. The origins of the esoteric doctrine are found in the mystery-teachings of beings from other and spiritual spheres, who incarnated in the early humanity of the third root-race of this fourth round of our globe, and taught the then intellectually nascent mankind the necessary certain fundamental principles or truths regarding the universe and the nature of the world surrounding us.

Ethics The theosophical teachings are essentially and wholly ethical. It is impossible to understand the sublime wisdom of the gods, the archaic wisdom-religion of the ancients, without the keenest realization of the fact that ethics run like golden threads throughout the entire system or fabric of doctrine and thought of the esoteric philosophy. Genuine occultism, divorced from ethics, is simply unthinkable because impossible. There is no genuine occultism which does not include the loftiest ethics that the moral sense of mankind can comprehend, and one cannot weigh with too strong an emphasis upon this great fact.

Ethics in the theosophical philosophy are not merely the products of human thought existing as a formulation of conventional rules proper for human conduct. They are founded on the very structure and character of the universe itself. The heart of the universe is wisdom-love, and these are intrinsically ethical, for there can be no wisdom without ethics, nor can love be without ethics, nor can there be ethics deprived of either love or wisdom.

The philosophic reason why the ancients set so much store by what was commonly known as *virtus* among the Latins, from which we have our modern word "virtue," is because by means of the teaching originating in the great Mystery schools, they knew that virtues, ethics, were the offspring of the moral instinct in human beings, who derived them in their turn from the heart of the universe — from the kosmic harmony. It is high time that the Occidental world should cast forever into the limbo of exploded superstitions the idea that ethics is merely conventional morality, a convenience invented by man to smooth the asperities and dangers of human intercourse.

Of course every scholar knows that the words morals and ethics come from the Latin and Greek respectively, as signifying the customs or habits which it is proper to follow in civilized communities. But this fact itself, which is unquestionable, is in a sense disgraceful, for it would almost seem that we had not yet brought forth a word adequately describing the instinct for right and truth and troth and justice and honor and wisdom and love which we today so feebly express by the words ethics or morals. "Theosophist is who Theosophy does," wrote H. P. Blavatsky, and wiser and nobler words she never wrote. No one can be a theosophist who does not feel ethically and think ethically and live ethically in the real sense that is hereinbefore described. (*See also* Morals)

Evolution As the word is used in theosophy it means the "unwrapping," "unfolding," "rolling out" of latent powers and faculties native to and inherent in the entity itself, its own essential characteristics, or more generally speaking, the powers and faculties of its own character: the Sanskrit word for this last conception is *svabhāva* (q.v.). Evolution, therefore, does not mean merely that brick is added to brick, or experience merely topped by another experience, or that variation is superadded on other variations — not at all; for this would make of man and of other entities mere aggregates of incoherent and unwelded parts, without an essential unity or indeed any unifying principle.

In theosophy evolution means that man has in him (as indeed have all other evolving entities) everything that the cosmos has because he is an inseparable part of it. He is its child; one cannot separate man from the universe. Everything that is in the universe is in him, latent or active, and evolution is the bringing forth of what is within; and, furthermore, what we call the surrounding milieu, circumstances — nature, to use the popular word — is merely the field of action on and in which these inherent qualities function, upon which they act and from which they receive the corresponding reaction, which action and reaction invariably become a stimulus or spur to further manifestations of energy on the part of the evolving entity.

There are no limits in any direction where evolution can be said to begin, or where we can conceive of it as ending; for evolution in the theosophical conception is but the process followed by the centers of consciousness or monads as they pass from eternity to eternity, so to say, in a beginningless and endless course of unceasing growth.

Growth is the key to the real meaning of the theosophical teaching of evolution, for growth is but the expression in detail of the general process of the unfolding of faculty and organ, which the usual word evolution includes. The only difference between evolution and growth is that the former is a general term, and the latter is a specific and particular phase of this procedure of nature.

Evolution is one of the oldest concepts and teachings of the archaic wisdom, although in ancient days the concept was usually expressed by the word emanation. There is indeed a distinction, and an important one, to be drawn between these two words, but it is a distinction arising rather in viewpoint than in any actual fundamental difference. Emanation is a distinctly more accurate and descriptive word for theosophists to use than evolution is, but unfortunately emanation is so ill-understood in the Occident, that perforce the accepted term is used to describe the process of interior growth expanding into and manifesting itself in the varying phases of the developing entity. Theosophists, therefore, are, strictly speaking, rather *emanationists* than *evolutionists*; and from this remark it becomes immediately obvious that the theosophist is not a Darwinist, although admitting that in certain secondary or tertiary senses and details there is a modicum of truth in Charles Darwin's theory adopted and adapted from the Frenchman Lamarck. The key to the meaning of evolution, therefore, in theosophy is the following: the core of every organic entity is a divine monad or spirit, expressing its faculties and powers through the ages in various vehicles which change by improving as the ages pass. These vehicles are not physical bodies alone, but also the interior sheaths of consciousness which together form man's entire constitution extending from the divine monad through the intermediate ranges of consciousness to the physical body. The evolving entity can become or show itself to be only what it already essentially is in itself — therefore evolution is a bringing out or unfolding of what already preexists, active or latent, within. (*See also* Involution)

Exoteric This word, when applied particularly to the great philosophical and religious systems of belief, does not mean false. The word merely means teachings of which the keys have not been openly given. The word seems to have originated in the Peripatetic School of Greece, and to have been born in the mind of Aristotle. Its contrast is "esoteric."

Exotericism — that is to say, the outward and popular formulation of religious and philosophic doctrines — *reveils* the truth; the self-assurance of ignorance, alas, always *reviles* the truth; whereas esotericism *reveals* the truth.

— F —

Fohat An extremely mystical term used in the occultism of Tibet for what in Sanskrit is called daivīprakṛiti (q.v.), which means "divine nature" or "primordial nature," and which also can be called "primordial light." In one sense of the word fohat may be considered as almost identical with the old mystical Greek eros, but fohat as a technical term contains within itself a far wider range of ideas than does the Greek term.

Fohat may be considered as the essence of kosmic electricity, provided, however, that in this definition we endow the term electricity with the attribute of consciousness; or, to put it more accurately, provided that we understand that the essence of electricity is indeed consciousness. It is ever-present and active from the primordial beginnings of a manvantara to its last end, nor does it then actually pass out of existence, but becomes quiescent or latent as it were, sleeping or dormant during the kosmic pralaya. In one sense of the word it may be called kosmic will, for the analogy with the conscious will in human beings is exceedingly close. It is the incessantly active, ever-moving, impelling or urging force in nature, from the beginning of the evolution of a universe or of a solar system to its end.

H. P. Blavatsky, quoting one of the ancient mystically occult works, says in substance: "Fohat is the steed and thought is the rider." If, however, we liken fohat to what the conscious will is in the human being, we must then think only of the lower or substantial parts — the prāṇic activities — of the human will, for behind the substantial parts stands always the directing and guiding consciousness. Fohat being incessantly active is therefore both formative and destructive, because it is through the ceaseless working of fohat that unending change continues — the passing of one phase of manifested existence to another phase, whether this manifested existence be a solar system or a planetary chain or a globe or human being or, indeed, any entity.

Fohat is as active among the electrons of an atom and among the atoms themselves as it is among the suns. In one sense it may be called the vital force of the universe, corresponding from this viewpoint to the prāṇic activity on all the seven planes of the human constitution.

— G —

Gāyatrī or **Sāvitrī** (Sanskrit) A verse of the *Ṛig-Veda* (iii.62.10) which from immemorial time in India has been surrounded with the attributes of quasi-divinity. The Sanskrit words of this verse are: *Tat savitur vareṇyam bhargo devasya dhīmahi, dhiyo yo nah prachodayāt.* Every orthodox Brāhmaṇa is supposed to repeat this archaic hymn, at least mentally, at both his morning and evening religious exercises or devotions. A translation in explanatory paraphrase, giving the essential esoteric meaning of the Gāyatrī or Sāvitrī, is the following: "Oh thou golden sun of most excellent splendor, illumine our hearts and fill our minds, so that we, recognizing our oneness with the Divinity which is the heart of the universe, may see the pathway before our feet, and tread it to those distant goals of perfection, stimulated by thine own radiant light."

Globe Every one of the physical globes that we see scattered over the fields of space is accompanied by six — really eleven — invisible and superior globes, forming what in theosophy is called a chain. This is the case with every sun or star, with every planet, and with every moon of every planet. It is likewise the case with the nebulae and the comets: all are septiform entities in manifestation; all have a sevenfold — indeed twelvefold — constitution, even as man has, who is a copy in the little of what the universe is in the great. The seven manifested globes for purposes of convenience are enumerated as A, B, C, D, E, F, and G; but reference is sometimes made more mystically to the globes from "A to Z," here hinting at but not specifying all the twelve globes of the chain.

The life-waves circle around these globes in seven great cycles which are called rounds. Each life-wave first enters globe A, runs through its life cycle there, and then passes on to globe B. Finishing its cycle on globe B, it passes on to globe C, and then to globe

D, the lowest of the manifested seven. In our own planetary chain, globe D is our earth. Three globes precede it on the downward arc, and three globes follow it on the ascending arc of evolution — referring here to the manifested seven.

The passing through or traversing of any one of these seven globes by the life-wave is a globe round; and during any one globe round on a globe, seven root-races are born, attain their efflorescence, and then pass away. (*See also* ROUND)

God The core of the core of a human being or of any other organic entity whatsoever is a kosmic spirit, a spark so to say of the kosmic flame of life. (*See also* INNER GOD)

Gods The old pantheons were builded upon an ancient and esoteric wisdom which taught, under the guise of a public mythology, profound secrets of the structure and operations of the universe which surrounds us. The entire human race has believed in gods, has believed in beings superior to men; the ancients all said that men are the "children" of these gods, and that from these superior beings, existent in the azure spaces, men draw all that in them is; and, furthermore, that men themselves, as children of the gods, are in their inmost essence divine beings linked forever with the boundless universe of which each human being, just as is the case with every other entity everywhere, is an inseparable part. This is a truly sublime conception.

One should not think of human forms when the theosophist speaks of the gods; we mean the *arūpa* — the "formless" — entities, beings of pure intelligence and understanding, relatively pure essences, relatively pure spirits, formless as we physical humans conceive form. The gods are the higher inhabitants of nature. They are intrinsic portions of nature itself, for they are its informing principles. They are as much subject to the *wills* and *energies* of still higher beings — call these wills and energies the "laws" of higher beings, if you will — as we are, and as are the kingdoms of nature below us.

The ancients put realities, *living beings*, in the place of laws which, as Occidentals use the term, are only abstractions — an expression for the *action of entities in nature*; the ancients did not cheat themselves so easily with words. They called them gods, spiritual entities. Not one single great thinker of the ancients, until the Christian era, ever talked about laws of nature, as if these laws were living entities, as if these abstractions were actual entities which did things. Did the *laws* of navigation ever navigate a ship? Does the *law* of gravity pull the planets together? Does it unite or pull the atoms together? This word laws is simply a mental abstraction signifying unerring action of conscious and semi-conscious energies in nature.

Guṇas or **Triguṇas** (Sanskrit) Differentiated matter is considered to possess or to have in occult philosophy three essential qualities or characteristics inherent in it, and their Sanskrit names are *sattva*, *rajas*, and *tamas* (*see also* each one of these three). These three are the guṇas or triguṇas.

Guru (Sanskrit) Sometimes *gurudeva*, "master divine." The word used in the old Sanskrit scriptures for teacher, preceptor. According to the beautiful teachings of the ancient wisdom, the guru acts as the midwife bringing to birth, helping to bring into the active life of the chela, the spiritual and intellectual parts of the disciple — the soul of the man. Thus the relationship between teacher and disciple is an extremely sacred one, because it is a tie which binds closely heart to heart, mind to mind. The idea is, again, that the latent spiritual potencies in the mind and heart of the learner shall receive such assistance in their development as the teacher can karmically give; but it does not mean that the teacher shall do the work that the disciple himself or herself must do. The learner or disciple must tread his own path, and the teacher cannot tread it for him. The teacher points the way, guides and aids, and the disciple follows the path.

Guru-paramparā (Sanskrit) This is a compound formed of *guru*, meaning "teacher," and a subordinate compound *param-parā*, the latter compound meaning "a row or uninterrupted series or succession." Hence *guru-paramparā* signifies an uninterrupted series or succession of teachers. Every Mystery school or esoteric college of ancient times had its regular and uninterrupted series or succession of teacher succeeding teacher, each one passing on to his successor the mystical authority and headship he himself had received from his predecessor.

Like everything else of an esoteric character in the ancient world, the guru-paramparā or succession of teachers faithfully copied what actually exists or takes place in nature herself, where a hierarchy with its summit or head is immediately linked on to a superior hierarchy as well as to an inferior one; and it is in this manner that the mystical circulations of the kosmos (q.v.), and the transmission of life or vital currents throughout the fabric or web of being is assured.

From this ancient fact and teaching of the Mystery schools came the greatly distorted Apostolic Succession of the Christian Church, a pale and feeble reflection in merely ecclesiastical government of a fundamental spiritual and mystical reality. The great Brotherhood of the sages and seers of the world, which in fact is the association of the Masters of Wisdom and Compassion headed by the Mahā-chohan, is the purest and most absolute form or example of the guru-paramparā existing on our earth today. (*See also* HERMETIC CHAIN)

— H —

Haṭha Yoga *See* YOGA

Heaven and Hell Every ancient exoteric religion taught that the so-called heavens are divided into steps or grades of ascending bliss and purity; and the so-called hells into steps or grades of increasing purgation or suffering. Now the esoteric doctrine or occultism teaches that the one is not a punishment, nor is the other strictly speaking a reward. The teaching is, simply, that each entity after physical death is drawn to the appropriate sphere to which the karmic destiny of the entity and the entity's own character and impulses magnetically attract it. As a man works, as a man sows, in his life, that and that only shall he reap after death. Good seed produces good fruit; bad seed, tares — and perhaps even nothing of value or of spiritual use follows a negative and colorless life.

After the second death (q.v.), the human monad "goes" to devachan — often called in theosophical literature the heaven-world. There are many degrees in devachan: the highest, the intermediate, and the lowest. What becomes of the entity, on the other hand, the lower human soul, that is so befouled and weighted with earth thought and the lower instincts that it cannot rise? There may be enough in it of the spirit nature to hold it together as an entity and enable it to become a reincarnating being, but it is foul, it is heavy; its tendency is consequently downwards. Can it therefore rise into a heavenly felicity? Can it go even into the lower realms of devachan and there enjoy its modicum of the beatitude, bliss, of everything that is noble and beautiful? No. There is an appropriate sphere for every degree of development of the ego-soul, and it gravitates to that sphere and remains there until it is thoroughly purged, until the sin has been washed out, so to say. These are the so-called hells, beneath even the lowest ranges of devachan; whereas the arūpa heavens are the highest parts of the devachan. Nirvāṇa is a very different thing from the heavens. (*See also* Kāma-Loka, Avīchi, Devachan, Nirvāṇa)

Hermetic Chain Among the ancient Greeks there existed a mystical tradition of a chain of living beings, one end of which included the divinities in their various grades or stages of divine authority and activities, and the other end of which ran downwards through inferior gods and heroes and sages to ordinary men, and to the beings below man. Each link of this living chain of beings inspired and instructed the chain below itself, thus transmitting and communicating from link to link to the end of the marvelous living chain, love and wisdom and knowledge concerning the secrets of the universe, eventuating in mankind as the arts and the sciences necessary for human life and civilization. This was mystically called the Hermetic Chain or the Golden Chain.

In the ancient Mysteries the teaching of the existence and nature of the Hermetic Chain was fully explained; it is a true teaching because it represents distinctly and clearly and faithfully true and actual operations of nature. More or less faint and distorted copies of the teaching of this Hermetic Chain or Golden Chain or succession of teachers were taken over by various later formal and exoteric sects, such as the Christian Church, wherein the doctrine was called the Apostolic Succession. In all the great Mystery schools of antiquity there was this succession of teacher following teacher, each one passing on the light to his successor as he himself had received it from his predecessor; and as long as this transmission of light was a reality, it worked enormous spiritual benefit among men. Therefore all such movements lived, flourished, and did great good in the world. These teachers were the messengers to men from the Great Lodge of the Masters of Wisdom and Compassion. (*See also* GURU-PARAMPARĀ)

Hierarchy The word hierarchy merely means that a scheme or system or state of delegated directive power and authority exists in a self-contained body, directed, guided, and taught by one having supreme authority, called the hierarch. The name is used by theosophists, by extension of meaning, as signifying the innumerable degrees, grades, and steps of evolving entities in the kosmos, and as applying to all parts of the universe; and rightly so, because every different part of the universe — and their number is simply countless — is under the vital governance of a divine being, of a god, of a spiritual essence; and all material manifestations are simply the appearances on our plane of the workings and actions of these spiritual beings behind it.

The series of hierarchies extends infinitely in both directions. If he so choose for purposes of thought, man may consider himself at the middle point, from which extends above him an unending series of steps upon steps of higher beings of all grades — growing constantly less material and more spiritual, and greater in all senses — towards an ineffable point. And there the imagination stops, not because the series itself stops, but because our thought can reach no farther out nor in. And similar to *this* series, an infinitely great series of beings and states of beings descends downwards (to use human terms) — downwards and downwards, until there again the imagination stops, merely because our thought can go no farther.

The summit, the acme, the flower, the highest point (or the hyparxis) of any series of animate and "inanimate" beings, whether we enumerate the stages or degrees of the series as seven or ten or twelve (according to whichever system we follow), is the divine unity for that series or hierarchy, and this hyparxis or highest being is again in its turn the lowest being of the hierarchy above it, and so extending onwards forever — each hierarchy manifesting one facet of the divine kosmic life, each hierarchy showing forth one thought, as it were, of the divine thinkers.

Various names were given to these hierarchies considered as series of beings. The generalized Greek hierarchy as shown by writers in periods preceding the rise of Christianity may be collected and enumerated as follows: (1) Divine; (2) Gods, or the divine-spiritual; (3) Demigods, sometimes called divine heroes, involving a very mystical doctrine; (4) Heroes proper; (5) Men; (6) Beasts or animals; (7) Vegetable world; (8) Mineral world; (9) Elemental world, or what was called the realm of Hades. The Divinity (or aggregate divine lives) itself is the hyparxis of this series of hierarchies, because each of these nine stages is itself a subordinate hierarchy. This (or any other) hierarchy of nine, hangs like a pendant jewel from the lowest hierarchy above it, which makes the tenth counting upwards, which tenth we can call the superdivine, the hyperheavenly, this tenth being the lowest stage (or the ninth, counting downwards) of still another hierarchy extending upwards; and so on, indefinitely.

One of the noblest of the theosophical teachings, and one of the most far-reaching in its import, is that of the hierarchical constitution of universal nature. This hierarchical structure of nature is so fundamental, so basic, that it may be truly called the structural framework of being. (*See also* PLANES)

Higher Triad The imperishable spiritual ego considered as a unity. It is the reincarnating part of man's constitution which clothes itself in each earth-life in a new personality or lower quaternary. The higher triad, speaking in the simplest fashion, is the unity of ātman, buddhi, and the higher manas; and the lower quaternary consists of the lower manas or kāma-manas, the prāṇa or vitality, the liṅga-śarīra or astral model-body, and the physical vehicle.

Another manner of considering the human constitution in its spiritual aspects is that viewed from the standpoint of consciousness, and in this latter manner the higher triad consists of the divine monad, the spiritual monad, and the higher human monad. The higher triad is often spoken of in a collective sense, and ignoring details of division, as simply the reincarnating monad, or more commonly the reincarnating ego, because this latter is rooted in the higher triad.

Many theosophists experience quite unnecessary difficulty in understanding why the human constitution should be at one time divided in one way and at another time divided in another way. The difficulty lies in considering these divisions as being absolute instead of relative, in other words, as representing watertight compartments instead of merely indefinite and convenient divisions. The simplest psychological division is probably that which divides the septenary constitution of man in three parts: an uppermost duad which is immortal, an intermediate duad which is conditionally immortal, and a lower triad which is unconditionally mortal. (See *Fundamentals of the Esoteric Philosophy*, 1st ed., pp. 167, 525; 2nd rev. ed., pp. 199, 601).

Home Galaxy *See* Milky Way

Home Universe *See* Milky Way

Hpho-Wa *See* Māyāvi-Rūpa

Human Ego The human ego is seated in that part of the human constitution which theosophists call the intermediate duad, manas-kāma. The part which is attracted below and is mortal is the lower human ego. The part which aspires upwards towards the buddhi and ultimately joins it is the higher human ego or reincarnating ego. The dregs of the human ego after the death of the human being and after the second death (q.v.) in the kāma-loka, remain in the astral spheres as the disintegrating kāma-rūpa or spook.

Human Monad In theosophical terminology the human monad is that part of man's constitution which is the root of the human ego. After death it allies itself with the upper duad, ātma-buddhi, and its inclusion within the bosom of the upper duad produces the source whence issues the Reincarnating Ego at its next rebirth. The monad per se is an upper duad alone, but the attributive adjective "human" is given to it on account of the reincarnating ego which it contains within itself after death. This last usage is rather popular and convenient than strictly accurate.

Human Soul The human soul, speaking generally, is the intermediate nature of man's constitution, and being an imperfect thing it is drawn back into incarnation on earth where it learns needed lessons in this sphere of the universal life.

Another term for the human soul is the ego — a usage more popular than accurate, because the human ego is the soul of the human soul so to speak, the human soul being its vehicle. The ego is that which says in each one of us, "I am *I*, not *you*!" It is the child of the immanent Self; and through its imprisonment in matter as a ray of the overruling immanent Self, it learns to reflect its consciousness back upon itself, thus obtaining cognition of itself as self-conscious and hetero-conscious, i.e., knowing itself, and knowing "non-self" or other selves.

Just as our higher and highest nature work through this human soul or intermediate nature of us, so does this last in its turn work and function through bodies or vehicles or sheaths of more or less etherealized matters which surround and enclose it, which are of course still lower than itself, and which therefore give it the means of contacting our own lower and lowest planes of matter; and these lower planes provide us with the vital-astral-physical parts of us. This human soul or intermediate nature manifests therefore as best it can through and by the astral-physical vehicle, the latter our body of human flesh.

In the theosophical classification, the human soul is divided into the higher human soul, composed of the lower buddhi and the higher manas — and the self corresponding to it is the bhūtātman, meaning the "self of that which has been" or the reincarnating ego — and the lower human soul, the lower manas and kāma, and the self corresponding to it is prāṇātman or astral personal ego, which is mortal.

Hypnotism Derived from a Greek word *hypnos*, which means "sleep," and strictly speaking the word hypnotism should be used only for those psychological-physiological phenomena in which the subject manifesting them is in a condition closely resembling sleep. The trouble is that in any attempt to study these various psychological powers of the human constitution it is found that they are many and of divers kinds; but the public, and even the technical experimenters, usually group all these psychological phenomena under the one word hypnotism, and therefore it is a misnomer. One of such powers, for instance, which is well known, is called fascination. Another shows a more or less complete suspension of the individual will and of the individual activities of him who is the sufferer from such psychological power, although in other respects he may show no signs of physical sleep. Another again — and this perhaps is the most important of all so far as actual dangers lie — passes under the name of suggestion, an exceedingly good name, because it describes the field of action of perhaps the most subtle and dangerous side-branch of the exercise of the general power or force emanating from the mind of the operator.

The whole foundation upon which this power rests lies in the human psychological constitution; and it can be easily and neatly expressed in a few words. It is the power emanating from one mind, which can affect another mind and direct or misdirect the latter's course of action. This is in nine hundred and ninety-nine times out of a thousand a wrong thing to do; and this fact would readily be understood by everybody did men know, as they should, the difference between the higher and the lower nature of man, the difference between his incorruptible, death-defying individuality, his spiritual nature, on the one hand; and, on the other hand, the brain-mind and all its train of weak and fugitive thoughts.

Anyone who has seen men and women in the state of hypnosis must realize not only how dangerous, how baleful and wrong it is, but also that it exemplifies the trance state perfectly. The reason is that the intermediate nature, or the psychomental apparatus, of the human being in this state has been displaced from its seat, in other words, is disjoined or dislocated; and there remains but the vitalized human body, with its more or less imperfect functioning of the brain cells and nervous apparatus. H. P. Blavatsky in her *Theosophical Glossary* writes: "It is the most dangerous of practices, morally and physically, as it interferes with the nerve-fluid and the nerves controlling the circulation in the capillary blood-vessels." (*See also* Mesmerism)

— I —

Idam *See* TAT

Illusion *See* MĀYĀ

Immortality A term signifying continuous existence or being; but this understanding of the term is profoundly illogical and contrary to nature, for there is nothing throughout nature's endless and multifarious realms of being and existence which remains for two consecutive instants of time exactly the same. Consequently, immortality is a mere figment of the imagination, an illusory phantom of reality. When the student of the esoteric wisdom once realizes that continuous progress, i.e., continuous change in advancement, is nature's fundamental procedure, he recognizes instantly that continuous remaining in an unchanging or immutable state of consciousness or being is not only impossible, but in the last analysis is the last thing that is either desirable or comforting. Fancy continuing immortal in a state of imperfection such as we human beings exemplify — which is exactly what the usual acceptance of this term immortality means. The highest god in highest heaven, although seemingly immortal to us imperfect human beings, is nevertheless an evolving, growing, progressing entity in its own sublime realms or spheres, and therefore as the ages pass leaves one condition or state to assume a succeeding condition or state of a nobler and higher type; precisely as the preceding condition or state had been the successor of another state before it.

Continuous or unending immutability of any condition or state of an evolving entity is obviously an impossibility in nature; and when once pondered over it becomes clear that the ordinary acceptance of immortality involves an impossibility. All nature is an unending series of changes, which means all the hosts or multitudes of beings composing nature, for every individual unit of these hosts is growing, evolving, i.e., continuously changing, therefore never immortal. Immortality and evolution are contradictions in terms. An evolving entity means a changing entity, signifying a continuous progress towards better things; and evolution therefore is a succession of state of consciousness and being after another state of consciousness and being, and thus throughout duration. The Occidental idea of static immortality or even mutable immortality is thus seen to be both repellent and impossible.

This doctrine is so difficult for the average Occidental easily to understand that it may be advisable once and for all to point out without mincing of words that just as complete death, that is to say, entire annihilation of consciousness, is an impossibility in nature, just so is continuous and unchanging consciousness in any one stage or phase of evolution likewise an impossibility, because progress or movement or growth is continuous throughout eternity. There are, however, periods more or less long of continuance in any stage or phase of consciousness that may be attained by an evolving entity; and the higher the being is in evolution, the more its spiritual and intellectual faculties have been evolved or evoked, the longer do these periods of continuous individual, or perhaps personal, quasi-immortality continue. There is, therefore, what may be called relative immortality, although this phrase is confessedly a misnomer.

Master KH in *The Mahatma Letters*, on pages 128–30, uses the phrase "panaeonic immortality" to signify this same thing that I have just called relative immortality, an immortality — falsely so called, however — which lasts in the cases of certain highly evolved monadic egos for the entire period of a manvantara, but which of necessity ends with the succeeding pralaya of the solar system. Such a period of time of continuous self-consciousness of so highly evolved a monadic entity is to us humans actually a relative immortality; but strictly and logically speaking it is no more immortality than is the ephemeral existence of a butterfly. When the solar manvantara comes to an end and the solar pralaya begins, even such highly evolved monadic entities, full-blown gods, are swept out of manifested self-conscious existence like the sere and dried leaves at the end of the autumn; and the divine entities thus passing out enter into still higher realms of superdivine activity, to reappear at the end of the pralaya and at the dawn of the next or succeeding solar manvantara.

The entire matter is, therefore, a highly relative one. What seems immortal to us humans would seem to be but as a wink of the eye to the vision of super-kosmic entities; while, on the other hand, the span of the average human life would seem to be immortal to a self-conscious entity inhabiting one of the electrons of an atom of the human physical body.

The thing to remember in this series of observations is the wondrous fact that consciousness from eternity to eternity is uninterrupted, although by the very nature of things undergoing continuous and unceasing change of phases in realization throughout endless duration. What men call unconsciousness is merely a form of consciousness which is too subtle for our gross brain-minds to perceive or to sense or to grasp; and, secondly, strictly speaking, what men call death, whether of a universe or of their own physical bodies, is but the breaking up of worn-out vehicles and the transference of consciousness to a higher plane. It is important to seize the spirit of this marvelous teaching, and not allow the imperfect brain-mind to quibble over words, or to pause or hesitate at difficult terms.

Individuality Theosophists draw a sharp and comprehensive distinction between individuality and personality. The individuality is the spiritual-intellectual and immortal part of us; deathless, at least for the duration of the kosmic manvantara — the root, the very essence of us, the spiritual sun within, our inner god. The personality is the veil, the mask, composed of various sheaths of consciousness through which the individuality acts.

The word individuality means that which cannot be divided, that which is simple and pure in the philosophical sense, indivisible, uncompounded, original. It is not heterogeneous; it is not composite; it is not builded up of other elements; it is the *thing in itself.* Whereas, on the contrary, the intermediate nature and the lower nature are composite, and therefore mortal, being builded up of elements other than themselves. Strictly speaking, individuality and monad are identical, but the two words are convenient because of the distinctions of usage contained in them; just as consciousness and self-consciousness are fundamentally identical, but convenient as words on account of the distinctions contained in them. (*See also* Monad)

Infinite A term meaning that which is not finite. The expression is used sometimes with almost absurd inaccuracy, and is one which in all probability representing as it does imperfect understanding could never be found in any of the great religious or philosophical systems of the ancients. Occidental writers of the past and present often use the word infinite as applying to beings or entities, such as in the expression "an infinite personal deity" — a ludicrous joining of contradictory and disparate words. The ancients rejected the phantom idea that this term involves, and used instead expressions such as the Boundless, or the Frontierless, or the Endless, whether speaking of abstract space or abstract time — the latter more properly called unending duration. (*See also* Absolute)

Initiates Those who have passed at least one initiation and therefore those who understand the mystery-teachings and who are ready to receive them at some future time in even larger measure. Please note the distinction between initiant and initiate. An initiant is one who is beginning or preparing for an initiation. An initiate is one who has successfully passed at least one initiation. It is obvious therefore that an initiate is always an initiant when he prepares for a still higher initiation.

The mystery-teachings were held as the most sacred treasure or possession that men could transmit to their descendants who were worthy postulants. The revelation of these mystery-doctrines under the seal of initiation, and under proper conditions to worthy depositaries, worked marvelous changes in the lives of those who underwent successfully the initiatory trials. It made men different from what they were before they received this spiritual and intellectual revelation. The facts are found in all the old religions and philosophies, if these are studied honestly. Initiation was always spoken of under the metaphor or figure of speech of "a new birth," a "birth into truth," for it was a spiritual and intellectual rebirth of the powers of the human spirit-soul, and could be called in all truth a birth of the soul into a loftier and nobler self-consciousness. When this happened, such men were called "initiates" or the reborn. In India, such reborn men were anciently called *dvija,* a Sanskrit word meaning "twice-born." In Egypt such initiates or reborn men were called "Sons of the Sun." In other countries they were called by other names.

Initiation In olden times there were seven — and even ten — degrees of initiation. Of these seven degrees, three consisted of teachings alone, which formed the preparation, the discipline, spiritual and mental and psychic and physical — what the Greeks called the *katharsis* or "cleansing." When the disciple was considered sufficiently cleansed, purified, disciplined, quiet mentally, tranquil spiritually, then he was taken into the fourth degree, which likewise consisted partly of teaching, but also in part of direct personal introduction by the old mystical processes into the structure and operations of the universe, by which means truth was gained by first-hand personal experience. In other words, to speak in plain terms, his spirit-soul, his individual consciousness, was assisted to pass into other planes and realms of being, and to know and to understand by the sheer process of *becoming them.* A man, a mind, an understanding, can grasp and see, and thereby know, only those things which *the individual entity itself is.*

After the fourth degree, there followed the fifth and the sixth and the seventh initiations, each in turn, and these consisted of teachings also; but more and more as the disciple progressed — and he was helped in this development more and more largely as he advanced farther — there was evolved forth in him the power and faculties still farther and more deeply to penetrate beyond the veils of māyā or illusion; until, having passed the seventh or last initiation of all of the manifest initiations, if we may call them that, he became one of those individuals whom theosophists call the mahātmas.

Inner God Mystics of all the ages have united in teaching this fact of the existence and ever-present power of an individual inner god in each human being, as the first principle or primordial energy governing the progress of man out of material life into the spiritual. Indeed, the doctrine is so perfectly universal, and is so consistent with everything that man knows when he reflects over the matter of his own spiritual and intellectual nature, that it is small wonder that this doctrine should have acquired foremost place in human religious and philosophical consciousness. Indeed, it may be called the very foundation-stone on which were builded the great systems of religious and philosophical thinking of the past; and rightly so, because this doctrine is founded on nature herself.

The inner god in man, man's own inner, essential divinity, is the root of him, whence flow forth in inspiring streams into the psychological apparatus of his constitution all the inspirations of genius, all the urgings to betterment. All powers, all faculties, all characteristics of individuality, which blossom through evolution into individual manifestation, are the fruitage of the working in man's constitution of those life-giving and inspiring streams of spiritual energy.

The radiant light which streams forth from that immortal center or core of our inmost being, which is our inner god, lightens the pathway of each one of us; and it is from this light that we obtain ideal conceptions. It is by this radiant light in our hearts that we can guide our feet towards an ever larger fulfilling in daily life of the beautiful conceptions which we as mere human beings dimly or clearly perceive, as the case may be.

The divine fire which moves through universal Nature is the source of the individualized divine fire coming from man's inner god.

The modern Christians of a mystical bent of mind call the inner god the Christ Immanent, the immanent Christos; in Buddhism it is called the living Buddha within; in Brahmanism it is spoken of as the Brahmā in his Brahmapura or Brahma-city, which is the inner constitution.

Hence, call it by what name you please, the reflective and mystical mind intuitively realizes that there works through him a divine flame, a divine life, a divine light, and that this by whatever name we may call it, is himself, his essential SELF. (*See also* GOD)

Inner Round *See* ROUND

Intermediate Nature To speak of man as a trichotomy, or as having a division into three parts — as in the Christian New Testament: a "natural" body, a psychical body, and a spiritual body — is a convenient expression, but it by no means sets forth in detail the entire economy of man's inner being.

Following then this trichotomy, there is first the divine-spiritual element in the human constitution which is man's own individual inner god; second, the soul or human monad, which is his human egoic self, his intermediate or psychical or second nature; third, all the composite lower part of him which although comprising several sheaths may be conveniently grouped under the one term vehicle or body. Gods, monads, and atoms collectively in nature are copied in the essential trichotomy of man, as spirit, soul, and body, and hence the latter is another way of saying man's divine-spiritual, intermediate soul, and astral-physical parts.

It is the intermediate nature, offspring of the divine spark, which enshrines the ray from the divine spark, its spiritual sun so to say, and steps it down into the ordinary mentality of man. It is this intermediate nature which reincarnates. The divine-spiritual part of man does not reincarnate, for this part of man has no need of learning the lessons that physical life can give: it is far above them all. But it is the intermediate part functioning through the various garments or sheaths of the inner man — these garments may be called astral or ethereal — which in this manner can reach down to and touch our earthly plane; and the physical body is the garment of flesh in touch with the physical world.

The intermediate nature is commonly called the human soul. It is an imperfect thing, and is that which comes back into incarnation, because it is drawn to this earth by attraction. It learns much needed lessons here, in this sphere of the universal life. (*See also* Principles of Man)

Invisible Worlds The ancient wisdom teaches that the universe is not only a living organism, but that physical human beings live in intimate connection, in intimate contact, with invisible spheres, with invisible and intangible realms, unknown to man because the physical senses are so imperfectly evolved that we neither see these invisible realms nor feel nor hear nor smell nor taste them, nor cognize them except by that much more highly evolved and subtle sensorium which men call the mind. These inner realms interpenetrate our physical sphere, permeate it, so that in our daily affairs as we go about our duties we actually pass through the dwellings, through the mountains, through the lakes, through the very beings, mayhap, of the entities of and dwelling in these invisible realms. These invisible realms are built of matter just as this our physical world is, but of a more ethereal matter than ours is; but we cognize them not at all with our physical senses. The explanation is that it is all a matter of differing rates of vibration of substances.

The reader must be careful not to confuse this theosophical teaching of inner worlds and spheres with what the modern Spiritism of the Occident has to say on the matter. The "Summerland" of the Spiritists in no wise resembles the actuality which the theosophical philosophy teaches of, the doctrine concerning the structure and operations of the visible and invisible kosmos. The warning seems necessary lest an unwary reader may imagine that the invisible worlds and spheres of the theosophical teachings are identic with the Summerland of the Spiritists, for it is not so.

Our senses tell us absolutely nothing of the far-flung planes and spheres which belong to the ranges and functionings of the invisible substances and energies of the universe; yet those inner and invisible planes and spheres are actually inexpressibly more important than what our physical senses tell us of the physical world, because these invisible planes are the *causal realms*, of which our physical world or universe, however far extended in space, is but the effectual or phenomenal or resultant production.

But while these inner and invisible worlds or planes or spheres are the fountainhead, ultimately, of all the energies and matters of the whole physical world, yet to an entity inhabiting these inner and invisible worlds or planes, these latter are as substantial and "real" — using the popular word — to that entity as our gross physical world is to us. Just as we know in our physical world various grades or conditions of energy and matter, from the physically grossest to the most ethereal, precisely after the same general plan do the inhabitants of these invisible and inner and to us superior worlds know and cognize their own grossest and also most ethereal substances and energies.

Man as well as all the other entities of the universe is inseparably connected with these worlds invisible.

Involution The reverse process or procedure of evolution. As evolution means the unfolding, the unwrapping, the rolling forth, of what already exists and is latent, so involution means the inwrapping, the infolding, the ingoing of what previously exists or has been unfolded, etc. Involution and evolution never in any circumstances can be even conceived of properly as operative the one apart from the other: every act of evolution is an act of involution, and vice versa. To illustrate, as spirit and matter are fundamentally one and yet eternally coactive and interactive, so involution and evolution are two names for two phases of the same procedure of growth, and are eternally coactive and interactive. As an example, the so-called descent of the monads into matter means an involution or involving or infolding of spiritual potencies into material vehicles which coincidently and contemporaneously, through the compelling urge of the infolding energies, unfold their own latent capacities, unwrap them, roll them forth; and this is the evolution of matter. Thus what is the involution of spirit is contemporaneously and *pari passu* the evolution of matter. Contrariwise, on the ascending or luminous arc when the involved monadic essences begin to rise towards their primordial spiritual source they begin to unfold or unwrap themselves as previously on the descending arc they had infolded or inwrapped themselves. But this process of unfolding or evolution of the monadic essences is contemporaneous with and *pari passu* with the infolding and inwrapping, the involution, of the material energies and powers.

Human birth and death are outstanding illustrations or examples of the same thing. The child is born, and as it grows to its full efflorescence of power it evolves or rolls forth certain inherent characteristics or energies or faculties, all derived from the human being's svabhāva or ego. Contrariwise, when the decline of human life begins, there is a slow infolding or inwrapping of these same facilities which thus seem gradually to diminish. These facilities and energies thus evolved forth in earth-life are the working of the innate spiritual and intellectual and psychical characteristics impelling and compelling the vehicular or body sides of the human constitution to express themselves as organs becoming more and more perfect as the child grows to maturity.

After death the process is exactly the reverse. The material or vehicular side of the being grows less and less strong and powerful, more and more involved, and becoming with every step in the process more dormant. But contemporaneously and coincidently the distinctly spiritual and intellectual powers and faculties themselves become released from the vehicles and begin to expand into ever larger efflorescence, attaining their maximum in the devachan. It is only the usual carelessness in accurate thinking that induces the idea that evolution is one distinct process acting alone, and that involution — about which by the way very little is heard — is another process acting alone. The two, as said above, are the two phases of activity of the evolving monads, and these phases exist contemporaneously at any moment, each of the two phases continually acting and interacting with the other phase. They are inseparable.

Just so with spirit and matter. Spirit is not something radically distinct from and utterly separate from matter. The two are fundamentally one, and the two are eternally coactive and interactive.

There are several terms in Sanskrit which correspond to what the theosophist means by evolution, but perhaps the best general term is *pravṛitti,* meaning to "revolve" or to "roll forwards," to unroll or to unwrap. Again, the reverse procedure or involution can probably best be expressed in Sanskrit by the term *nivṛitti,* meaning "rolling backwards" or "inwrapping" or "infolding." A term which is frequently interchangeable with evolution is emanation. (*See also* EVOLUTION)

Īśvara (Sanskrit) Īśvara means "lord," and is a term which is frequently applied in Hindu mythology not only to kosmic divinities, but to the expression of the cosmic spirit in the human being. Consequently, when reference is had to the individual human being, Īśvara is the divine individualized spirit in man — man's own personal god. It may be otherwise described as the divine ego, the child of the divine monad in a man, and in view of this fact also could be used with reference to the dhyāni-buddha or to the immanent Christ in a man. In India it is a title frequently given to Śiva and other gods of the Hindu pantheon.

— J —

Jāgrat (Sanskrit) The state of consciousness when awake, as opposed to *svapna,* the dreaming-sleeping state of consciousness, and different again from *sushupti* when the human consciousness is plunged into profound self-oblivion. The highest of all the states into which the consciousness may cast itself, or be cast, is the *turīya* ("fourth"), which is the highest state of *samādhi,* and is almost a nirvāṇic condition.

All these states or conditions of the consciousness are affections or phases of the constitution of man, and of beings constructed similarly to man. The waking state, or jāgrat, is the state or condition of consciousness normal to the imbodied human being when not asleep. Svapna is the state of consciousness more or less freed from the sheath of the body and partially awake in the astral realms, higher or lower as the case may be. Sushupti is the state of self-oblivion into which the human being is plunged when the percipient consciousness enters into the purely mānasic condition, which is self-oblivion for the relatively impotent brain-mind; whereas the turīya state, which is a practical annihilation of the ordinary human consciousness, is an attainment of union with ātma-buddhi overshadowing or working through the higher manas. Actually, therefore, it is becoming at one with the monadic essence.

Jīva (Sanskrit) This is a word meaning essentially a *living* being per se, apart from any attributes or qualities that such living being may have or possess. It therefore is the exactly proper equivalent of the theosophical term monad. In one sense, therefore, jīva could be also used for a life-atom, provided that the emphasis be laid on the word *life,* or rather life-entity — not an "atom of life," but a being whose essence is pure living individuality. Monad in its divine-spiritual essence, and life-atom in its prāṇic-astral-physical being — such is a jīva; and between these two extremes are the numerous planes or sheaths on and in which the individualized consciousness works.

Jīvanmukta (Sanskrit) A highly mystical and philosophical word which means "a freed jīva," signifying a human being, or an entity equivalent in evolutionary development to a human being, who has attained freedom or release as an individualized monad from the enthralling chains and attractions of the material spheres.

A jīvanmukta is not necessarily without body; and, as a matter of fact, the term is very frequently employed to signify the loftiest class of initiates or Adepts who through evolution have risen above the binding attractions or magnetism of the material spheres. The term is frequently used for a mahātma, whether imbodied or disimbodied, and also occasionally as a descriptive term for a nirvāṇī — one who has reached nirvāṇa during life. Were the nirvāṇī "without body," the mystical and technical meaning of jīvanmukta would hardly apply. Consequently, jīvanmukta may briefly be said to be a human being who lives in the highest portions of his constitution in full consciousness and power even during earth-life.

Jīvātman (Sanskrit) An expressive word having much the same significance as jīva, but with emphasis laid upon the last element of the compound, ātman, "self." Jīvātman is perhaps a better term for monad even than jīva is, because it carries the clear idea of the monad in which the individual self is predominant over all other monadic attributes. One may perhaps describe it by a paraphrase as "the essential *self* or individuality of the monad."

Jīvātman is also a term sometimes used for the universal life; but this definition, while correct in a way, is rather confusing because suggesting similarity if not identity with paramātman. Paramātman (q.v.) is the Brahman or universal spirit of a solar system, for instance; and paramātman is therefore the converging point of a kosmic consciousness in which all the hosts of jīvātmans unite as in their hierarchical head. The jīvātmans of any hierarchy are like the rays from the paramātman, their divine-spiritual sun. The jīvātman, therefore, in the case of the human being, or indeed of any other evolving entity, is the spiritual monad, or better perhaps the spiritual ego of that monad.

— K —

Kabala *See* Qabbālāh

Kali Yuga *See* Yuga

Kalpa (Sanskrit) This word comes from a verb-root *kḷrip,* meaning "to be in order"; hence a "period of time," or a "cycle of time." Sometimes a kalpa is called the period of a mahā-manvantara — or "great manvantara" — after which the globes of a planetary chain no longer go into obscuration or repose, as they periodically do, but die utterly. A kalpa is also called a Day of Brahmā, and its length is 4,320,000,000 years. Seven rounds form a Day of Brahmā, or a planetary manvantara. (*See also* Brahmā, Manvantara)

Seven planetary manvantaras (or planetary cycles, each cycle consisting of seven rounds) form one solar kalpa (or solar manvantara), or seven Days of Brahmā — a week of Brahmā.

The difficulty that many Western students have had in understanding this word lies in the fact that it is unavoidably a "blind," because it does not apply with exclusive meaning to the length of one time period alone. Like the English word age, or the English phrase time period, the word kalpa may be used for several different cycles. There is likewise the mahā-kalpa or "great kalpa," which frequently is the name given to the vast time period contained in a complete solar manvantara or complete solar pralaya.

Kāma (Sanskrit) "Desire"; the fourth substance-principle of which man's constitution is composed. Kāma is the driving or impelling force in the human constitution; per se it is colorless, neither good nor bad, and is only such as the mind and soul direct its use. It is the seat of the living electric impulses, desires, aspirations, considered in their energic aspect. Usually however, although there is a divine kāma as well as an infernal one, this word is restricted, and wrongly so, to evil desire almost exclusively.

Kāma-Loka (Sanskrit) A compound which can be translated as "desire world," which is accurate enough, but only slightly descriptive. It is a semi-material plane or rather world or realm, subjective and invisible to human beings as a rule, which surrounds and also encloses our physical globe. It is the habitat or dwelling-place of the astral forms of dead men and other dead beings — the realm of the kāma-rūpas or desire-bodies of defunct humans. "It is the Hades," as H. P. Blavatsky says, "of the ancient Greeks, and the Amenti of the Egyptians, the land of Silent Shadows."

It is in the kāma-loka that the second death (q.v.) takes place, after which the freed upper duad of the human being that was enters the devachan. The highest regions of the kāma-loka blend insensibly into the lowest regions or realms of the devachan; and, conversely, the grossest and lowest regions of the kāma-loka blend insensibly into the highest regions of the avīchi (q.v.).

When the physical body breaks up at death, the astral elements of the excarnate entity remain in the kāma-loka or "shadow world," with the same vital centers as in physical life clinging within them, still vitalizing them; and here certain processes take place. The lower human soul that is befouled with earth-thought and the lower instincts cannot easily rise out of the kāma-loka, because it is foul, it is heavy; and its tendency is consequently downwards. It is in the kāma-loka that the processes of separation of the monad from the kāma-rūpic spook or phantom take place; and when this separation is complete, which is the second death above spoken of, then the monad receives the reincarnating ego within its bosom, wherein it enjoys its long rest of bliss and recuperation. If, contrariwise, the entity in the kāma-loka is so heavy with evil and is so strongly attracted to earth spheres that the influence of the monad cannot withdraw the reincarnating ego from the kāma-rūpa, then the latter with its befouled soul sinks lower and lower and may even enter the avīchi. If the influence of the monad succeeds, as it usually does, in bringing about the second death, then the kāma-rūpa becomes a mere phantom or kāma-rūpic spook, and begins instantly to decay and finally vanishes away, its component life-atoms pursuing each one the road whither its attractions draw it.

Kāma-Rūpa (Sanskrit) A compound word signifying "desire body." It is that part of man's inner constitution in which dwell or inhere the various desires, affections, hates, loves — in short, the various mental and psychical energies. After death it becomes the vehicle in the astral worlds of the higher principles of the man that was. But these higher principles are nevertheless scarcely conscious of the fact, because the rupture of the golden cord of life at the moment of the physical death plunges the cognizing *personal* entity into a merciful stupor of unconsciousness, in which stupor it remains a longer or shorter period depending upon its qualities of spirituality or materiality. The more spiritual the man was the longer the period of merciful unconsciousness lasts, and vice versa.

After death, as has been frequently stated elsewhere, there occurs what is called the second death, which is the separation of the immortal part of the second or intermediate duad from the lower portions of this duad, which lower portions remain as the kāma-rūpa in the etheric or higher astral spheres which are intermediate between the devachanic and the earthly spheres. In time this kāma-rūpa gradually fades out in its turn, its life-atoms at such dissolution passing on to their various and unceasing peregrinations.

It is this kāma-rūpa which legend and story in the various ancient world religions or philosophies speak of as the shade, and which it has been customary in the Occident to call the spook or ghost. It is, in short, all the mortal elements of the human soul that was. The kāma-rūpa is an exact astral duplicate, in appearance and mannerism, of the man who died; it is his eidolon (q.v.) or "image." (*See also* SECOND DEATH)

Kāraṇa-Śarīra (Sanskrit) A compound signifying "cause body" or "causal body," the instrument or principle or causal element in man's constitution, and inferentially in the constitution of any other reimbodying entity, which brings about not merely the reproduction in imbodied form of such entity, but likewise its evolution during a manvantara through an unending series of reimbodiments. (*See also* CAUSAL BODY, KĀRAṆOPĀDHI)

Kāraṇopādhi (Sanskrit) A compound meaning the "causal instrument" or "instrumental cause" in the long series of reimbodiments to which human and other reimbodying entities are subject. *Upādhi*, the second element of this compound, is often translated as "vehicle"; but while this definition is accurate enough for popular purposes, it fails to set forth the essential meaning of the word which is rather "disguise," or certain natural properties or constitutional characteristics supposed to be the disguises or clothings or masks in and through which the spiritual monad of man works, bringing about the repetitive manifestations upon earth of certain functions and powers of this monad, and, indeed, upon the other globes of the planetary chain; and, furthermore, intimately connected with the peregrinations of the monad through the various spheres and realms of the solar kosmos. In one sense of the word, therefore, kāraṇopādhi is almost interchangeable with the thoughts set forth under the term māyā (q.v.), or the illusory disguises through which spirit works, or rather through which spiritual monadic entities work and manifest themselves.

Kāraṇopādhi, as briefly explained under the term "causal body," is dual in meaning. The first and more easily understood meaning of this term shows that the cause bringing about reimbodiment is *avidyā*, nescience rather than ignorance; because when a reimbodying entity through repeated reimbodiments in the spheres of matter has freed itself from the entangling chains of the latter, and has risen into self-conscious recognition of its own divine powers, it thereby shakes off the chains or disguises of māyā and becomes what is called a jīvanmukta (q.v.). It is only imperfect souls, or rather monadic souls, speaking in a general way, which are obliged by nature's cyclic operations and laws to undergo the repetitive reimbodiments on earth and elsewhere in order that the lessons of self-conquest and mastery over all the planes of nature may be achieved. As the entity advances in wisdom and knowledge, and in the acquiring of self-conscious sympathy for all that is, in other words, as it grows more and more like unto its divine-spiritual counterpart, the less is it subject to avidyā. It is, in a sense, the seeds of kāma-manas left in the fabric or being of the reincarnating entity, which act as the *kāraṇa* or reproducing cause, or instrumental cause, of such entity's reincarnations on earth.

The higher kāraṇopādhi, however, although in operation similar to the lower kāraṇopādhi, or kāraṇa-śarīra just described, nevertheless belongs to the spiritual-intellectual part of man's constitution, and is the reproductive energy inherent in the spiritual monad bringing about its re-emergence after the solar pralaya into the new activities and new series of imbodiments which open with the dawn of the solar manvantara following upon the solar pralaya just ended. This latter kāraṇopādhi or kāraṇa-śarīra, therefore, is directly related to the element-principle in man's constitution called buddhi — a veil, as it were, drawn over the face or around the being of the monadic essence, much as prakṛiti surrounds Purusha, or pradhāna surrounds Brahman, or mūlaprakṛiti surrounds and is the veil or disguise or śakti of parabrahman. Hence, in the case of man, this kāraṇopādhi or causal disguise or vehicle corresponds in a general way to the buddhi-manas, or spiritual soul, in which the spiritual monad works and manifests itself.

It should be said in passing that the doctrine concerning the functions and operations of buddhi in the human constitution is extremely recondite, because in buddhi lie the causal impulses or urges bringing about the building of the constitution of man, and which, when the latter is completed, and when forming man as a septenary entity, express themselves as the various strata or qualities of the auric egg (q.v.).

Finally, the kāraṇa-śarīra, the kāraṇopādhi or causal body, is the vehicular instrumental form or instrumental body-form, produced by the working of what is perhaps the most mysterious principle or element, mystically speaking, in the constitution not only of man, but of the universe — the very mysterious spiritual bīja (q.v.).

The kāraṇopādhi, the kāraṇa-śarīra or causal body, is explained with minor differences of meaning in various works of Hindu philosophy; but all such works must be studied with the light thrown upon them by the great wisdom-teaching of the archaic ages, esoteric theosophy. The student otherwise runs every risk of being led astray.

I might add that the sushupti state or condition, which is that of deep dreamless sleep, involving entire insensibility of the human consciousness to all exterior impressions, is a phase of consciousness through which the adept must pass, although consciously pass in his case, before reaching the highest state of samādhi, which is the turīya state. According to the Vedānta philosophy, the turīya (meaning "fourth") is the fourth state of consciousness into which the full adept can self-consciously enter and wherein he becomes one with the kosmic Brahman. The Vedāntists likewise speak of the ānandamaya-kośa, which they describe as being the innermost disguise or frame or vehicle surrounding the ātmic consciousness. Thus we see that the ānandamaya-kośa and the kāraṇa-śarīra, or kāraṇopādhi, and the buddhi in conjunction with the mānasic ego, are virtually identical.

The author has been at some pains to set forth and briefly to develop the various phases of occult and esoteric theosophical thought given in this article, because of the many and various misunderstandings and misconceptions concerning the nature, characteristics, and functions of the kāraṇa-śarīra or causal body.

Karma (*Karman,* Sanskrit) This is a noun-form coming from the root *kṛi* meaning "to do," "to make." Literally *karma* means "doing," "making," action. But when used in a philosophical sense, it has a technical meaning, and this technical meaning can best be translated into English by the word consequence. The idea is this: When an entity acts, he acts from within; he acts through an expenditure in greater or less degree of his own native energy. This expenditure of energy, this outflowing of energy, as it impacts upon the surrounding milieu, the nature around us, brings forth from the latter perhaps an instantaneous or perhaps a delayed reaction or rebound. Nature, in other words, reacts against the impact; and the combination of these two — of energy acting upon nature and nature reacting against the impact of that energy — is what is called karma, being a combination of the two factors. Karma is, in other words, essentially a chain of causation, stretching back into the infinity of the past and therefore necessarily destined to stretch into the infinity of the future. It is unescapable, because it is in universal nature, which is infinite and therefore everywhere and timeless; and sooner or later the reaction will inevitably be felt by the entity which aroused it.

It is a very old doctrine, known to all religions and philosophies, and since the renascence of scientific study in the Occident has become one of the fundamental postulates of modern coordinated knowledge. If you toss a pebble into a pool, it causes ripples in the water, and these ripples spread and finally impact upon the bank surrounding the pool; and, so modern science tells us, the ripples are translated into vibrations, which are carried outward into infinity. But at every step of this natural process there is a corresponding reaction from every one and from all of the myriads of atomic particles affected by the spreading energy.

Karma is in no sense of the word fatalism on the one hand, nor what is popularly known as chance, on the other hand. It is essentially a doctrine of free will, for naturally the entity which initiates a movement or action — spiritual, mental, psychological, physical, or other — is responsible thereafter in the shape of consequences and effects that flow therefrom, and sooner or later recoil upon the actor or prime mover.

Since everything is interlocked and interlinked and interblended with everything else, and no thing and no being can live unto itself alone, other entities are of necessity, in smaller or larger degree, affected by the causes or motions initiated by any individual entity; but such effects or consequences on entities, other than the prime mover, are only indirectly a morally compelling power, in the true sense of the word moral.

An example of this is seen in what the theosophist means when he speaks of family karma as contrasted with one's own individual karma; or national karma, the series of consequences pertaining to the nation of which he is an individual; or again, the racial karma pertaining to the race of which the individual is an integral member. Karma cannot be said either to punish or to reward in the ordinary meaning of these terms. Its action is unerringly just, for being a part of nature's own operations, all karmic action ultimately can be traced back to the kosmic heart of harmony which is the same thing as saying pure consciousness-spirit. The doctrine is extremely comforting to human minds, inasmuch as man may carve his own destiny and indeed must do so. He can form it or deform it, shape it or misshape it, as he wills; and by acting with nature's own great and underlying energies, he puts himself in unison or harmony therewith and therefore becomes a co-worker with nature as the gods are.

Khe-Chara (*Khecara,* Sanskrit) "Ether-goer" or sometimes rendered as "sky-walker." The name used in the mystical and philosophical literature of Hindustan to signify one of the *siddhis* or psychospiritual powers that belong to yogis of advanced grade, or to initiates. It is, in fact, nothing more than what in Tibet is called hpho-wa, the projection of the māyāvi-rūpa (q.v.) to any part of the earth's surface or, indeed, farther than that, and the doing of this at will.

Kosmic Life All the great religions and philosophies of past times, all the ancient sciences likewise, taught the fact of the existence of inner, invisible, intangible, but causal realms, as the foundation and background of these various systems. According to them all, our physical world is but the outer shell or garment or veil of other worlds which are inner, vital, alive, and causal, which in their aggregate imbody the kosmic life. This kosmic life is not a person, not an individualized entity. It is far, far different from any such merely human conception, because it is infinite, boundless, beginningless, endless, coextensive with infinity, coextensive with eternity. The kosmic life is in very truth the ultimate reality behind and within all that is.

All the energies and matters in our world are really only various and innumerable manifestations of the kosmic life existing in truly infinitely large variety. The kosmic life, therefore, is, as said, the reality behind all the infinitely varied hosts of entities and things. But this reality is no personal or individualized Deity. It is precisely what theosophy calls it: the boundless and, in its totality, incomprehensible life-substance-consciousness.

Kosmos (Greek) A word meaning "arrangement"; that which was arranged and kept along the lines and rules of harmony, the arrangement of the universe. Kosmos, therefore, is virtually interchangeable with universe. It must be distinctly understood that kosmos and universe, when employed in the esoteric philosophy, signify above everything else the indwelling boundless life expressing itself in its multimyriad entities and forms producing the amazing variety, and unity in diversity, that we see around us. (*See also* COSMOS)

Kṛita Yuga or **Satya Yuga** *See* YUGA

Kshatriya (Sanskrit) The warrior, the administrator, the king, the prince, in short, the world of officialdom, etc.; the second of the four grades or classes, social and political, of the early civilizations of Hindustan in the Vedic Period. (*See also* BRĀHMAṆA, VAIŚYA, ŚŪDRA)

Kumāra(s) *See* AGNISHVĀTTAS

Kumbhaka (Sanskrit) An extremely dangerous practice belonging to the haṭha yoga system. It consists in retaining the breath by shutting the mouth and holding the nostrils closed with the fingers of the right hand. All these breathing exercises of whatever kind are attended with the utmost physiological danger to those who attempt to practice them, unless under the skilled guidance of a genuine Adept; and their practice is virtually forbidden, at least in the first few degrees, to all chelas of genuinely occult or esoteric schools. Indeed, except in rare instances, and for extraordinary reasons, the chela of a true Master of Wisdom will have no need to practice these haṭha yoga exercises, for the whole purpose of esoteric training is to evolve forth the faculties and powers of the inner divinity, and not to gain minor and often misleading powers of small range which are occasionally acquired by following the haṭha yoga physiologic and physical practices.

Kuṇḍalinī or **Kuṇḍalinī-Śakti** (Sanskrit) A term whose essential meaning is "circular" or "winding" or "spiral" or "coiling" action, or rather energy, and signifies a recondite power in the human constitution. Kuṇḍalinī-śakti is derivative of one of the elemental forces of nature. It works in and through, in the case of man, his auric egg (q.v.), and expresses itself in continuous action in many of the most familiar phenomena of existence even when man himself is unconscious of it. In its higher aspect Kuṇḍalinī is a power or force following winding or circular pathways carrying or conveying thought and force originating in the higher triad. Abstractly, in the case of man it is of course one of the fundamental energies or qualities of the prāṇas. Unskilled or unwise attempts to interfere with its normal working in the human body may readily result in insanity or malignant or enfeebling disease.

— L —

Ladder of Life A term frequently found in theosophical literature, briefly and neatly expressing the ascending grades or stages of manifested existences in the universe. In one sense the term ladder of life is interchangeable with the other terms, the Hermetic Chain (q.v.) or the Golden Chain.

The universe is imbodied consciousnesses; and these imbodied consciousnesses exist in a practically infinite gradation of varying degrees of perfection — a real ladder of life, or stair of life, stretching endlessly in either direction, for our imagination can conceive of no limits except a hierarchical one; and such hierarchical limitation is but spacial and not actual, qualitative and formal. This ladder of life is marked at certain intervals by landing places, so to say, which are what theosophists call the different planes of being — the different spheres of consciousness, to put the thought in another manner.

Lanoo A word used in old Asiatic mystical training-schools for "disciple." (*See also* Chela)

Laya-Center A "point of disappearance" — which is the Sanskrit meaning. *Laya* is from the Sanskrit root *lī,* meaning "to dissolve," "to disintegrate," or "to vanish away." A laya-center is the mystical *point* where a thing disappears from one plane and passes onwards to reappear on another plane. It is that point or spot — any point or spot — in space, which, owing to karmic law, suddenly becomes the center of active life, first on a higher plane and later descending into manifestation through and by the laya-centers of the lower planes. In one sense a laya-center may be conceived of as a canal, a channel, through which the vitality of the superior spheres pours down into, and inspires, inbreathes into, the lower planes or states of matter, or rather of substance. But behind all this vitality there is a directive and driving force. There are mechanics in the universe, mechanics of many degrees of consciousness and power. But behind the pure mechanic stands the spiritual-intellectual mechanician.

Finally, a laya-center is the point where substance rebecomes homogeneous. Any laya-center, therefore, of necessity exists in and on the critical line or stage dividing one plane from another. Any hierarchy, therefore, contains within itself a number of laya-centers. (*See also* HIERARCHY)

Left-hand Path *See* RIGHT-HAND PATH

Life-Atom A learning, evolving entity, each one a unit in one or other of the numberless hosts or hierarchies of them which exist. A life-atom is a vital individualized vehicle or body of a spiritual monad, which latter is the consciousness-center, the ultimate, noblest, highest, finest part of us. The heart of every life-atom is a spiritual monad. Life-atoms are young gods, embryo gods, and are, therefore, in a continuous process of self-expressing themselves on the planes of matter.

A life-atom may be briefly said to be the ensouling power in every primary or ultimate particle. An atom of physical matter is ensouled by such a life-atom, which is its prāṇic-astral-vital primary, the life-atom of it. The life-atom is not the physical atom, which latter is but its garment or vehicle and is compounded of physical matter only, which breaks up when its term of life has run, and which will return again in order to reimbody itself anew through the instrumentality and by the innate force or energy latent in its ensouling primary, the life-atom.

In other words, the life-atom has a house of life, and this house of life is its body or physical atom; and the life-atom itself is the lowest expression of the monadic light within that atomic house.

Life-Atoms The physical body is composed essentially of energy, of energies rather, in the forms that are spoken of in modern physical science as electrons and protons. These are in constant movement; they are incessantly active, and are what theosophists call the imbodiments or manifestations of *life-atoms.* These life-atoms are inbuilt into man's body during the physical life which he leads on earth, although they are not derivative from outside, but spring forth from within himself — at least a great majority of them are such. This is equivalent to saying that they compose both his physical as well as his intermediate nature, which latter is obviously higher than the physical.

When the man dies — that is to say, when the physical body dies — its elements pass, each and all, into their respective and appropriate spheres: some into the soil, to which those that go there are drawn by magnetic affinity, an affinity impressed upon their life-energies by the man when alive, whose overshadowing will and desires, whose overlordship and power, gave them that direction. Others pass into the vegetation from the same reason that the former are impelled to the mineral kingdom; others pass into the various beasts with which they have, at the man's death, magnetic affinity, psychic affinity more accurately, an affinity which the man has impressed upon them by his desires and various impulses; and those which take this path go to form the interior or intermediate apparatus of the beasts into which they pass. So much for the course pursued by the life-atoms of the man's lowest principles.

But there are other life-atoms belonging to him. There are life-atoms, in fact, belonging to the sphere of each one of the seven principles of man's constitution. This means that there are life-atoms belonging to his intermediate nature and to his spiritual nature and to all grades intermediate between these two higher parts of him. And in all cases, as the monad "ascends" or "rises" through the spheres, as he goes step by step higher on his wonderful postmortem journey, on each such step he discards or casts off the life-atoms belonging to each one of these steps or stages of the journey. With each step, he leaves behind the more material of these life-atoms until, when he has reached the culmination of his wonderful postmortem peregrination, he is, as Paul of the Christians said, living in "a spiritual body" — that is to say, he has become a spiritual energy, a monad.

Nature permits no absolute standing still for anything, anywhere. All things are full of life, full of energy, full of movement; they are both energy and matter, both spirit and substance; and these two are fundamentally one — phases of the underlying reality, of which we see but the māyā or illusory forms.

The life-atoms are actually the offspring or the off-throwings of the interior principles of man's constitution. It is obvious that the life-atoms which ensoul the physical atoms in man's body are as numerous as the atoms which they ensoul; and there are almost countless hosts of them, decillions upon decillions of them, in practically incomputable numbers. Each one of these life-atoms is a being which is living, moving, growing, never standing still — evolving towards a sublime destiny which ultimately becomes divinity.

Life-Wave This is a term which means the collective hosts of monads, of which hosts there are seven or ten, according to the classification adopted. The monad is a *spiritual ego,* a consciousness-center, being in the spiritual realms of the universal life what the life-atoms are in the lower planes of form. These monads and life-atoms collectively are the seven (or ten) life-waves — these monads with the life-atoms in and through which they work; these life-atoms having remained, when the former planetary chain went into pralaya, in space as kosmic dust on the physical plane, and as corresponding life-atoms or life-specks of differentiated matter on the intermediate planes above the physical. Out of the working of the monads as they come down into matter — or rather through and by the monadic rays permeating the lower planes of matter — are the globes builded. The seven (or ten) life-waves or hosts of monads consist of monads in seven (or ten) degrees of advancement for each host.

When the hosts of beings forming the life-wave — the life-wave being composed of the entities derived from a former but now dead planet, in our case the moon — find that the time has arrived for them to enter upon their own particular evolutionary course, they cycle downwards as a life-wave along the planetary chain that has been prepared for them by the three hosts of elementary beings, of the three primordial elementary worlds, the forerunners of the life-wave, yet integral parts of it. This life-wave passes seven times in all around the seven spheres of our planetary chain, at first cycling down the shadowy arc through all the seven elements of the kosmos, gathering experience in each one of them; each particular entity of the life-wave, no matter what its grade or kind — spiritual, psychic, astral, mental, divine — advancing, until at the bottom of the arc, when the middle of the fourth round is attained, they feel the end of the downward impulse. Then begins the upward impulse, the reascent along the luminous arc upwards, towards the source from which the life-wave originally came.

Liṅga-Śarīra (Sanskrit) *Liṅga* is a word which means "characteristic mark," hence "model," "pattern." *Śarīra,* "form," from a verb-root *śṛī,* meaning "to molder" or "to waste away," the word thus signifying "impermanence."

The sixth substance-principle, counting downwards, of which man's constitution is composed. The model-body, popularly called astral body, because it is but slightly more ethereal than the physical body, and is in fact the model or framework around which the physical body is builded, and from which, in a sense, the physical body flows or develops as growth proceeds.

At death the liṅga-śarīra or model-body remains in the astral realms and finally fades out, dissolving *pari passu,* atom by atom, with the atoms of the physical corpse. These astral realms are not one single plane, but a series of planes growing gradually more ethereal or spiritual as they approach the inward spheres of nature's constitution or structure. The liṅga-śarīra is formed before the body is formed, and thus serves as a model or pattern around which the physical body is molded and grows to maturity; it is as mortal as is the physical body, and disappears with the physical body.

Lipika(s) (Sanskrit) This word comes from the verb-root *lip*, meaning "to write"; hence the word lipikas means the "scribes." Mystically, they are the celestial recorders, and are intimately connected with the working of karma, of which they are the agents. They are the karmic "Recorders or Annalists, who impress on the (to us) invisible tablets of the Astral Light, 'the great picture-gallery of eternity,' a faithful record of every act, and even thought, of man [and indeed of all other entities and things], of all that was, is, or ever will be, in the phenomenal Universe" (*The Secret Doctrine* 1:104).

Their action although governed strictly by kosmic consciousness is nevertheless rigidly automatic, for their work is as automatic as is the action of karma itself. They are entities as a matter of fact, but entities which work and act with the rigid automatism of the kosmic machinery, rather than like the engineer who supervises and changes the running of his engines. In one sense they may perhaps better be called kosmic energies — a most difficult matter to describe.

Logos (Greek) In old Greek philosophy the word *logos* was used in many ways, of which the Christians often sadly misunderstood the profoundly mystical meaning. Logos is a word having several applications in the esoteric philosophy, for there are different kinds or grades of logoi, some of them of divine, some of them of a spiritual character; some of them having a cosmic range, and others ranges much more restricted. In fact, every individual entity, no matter what its evolutionary grade on the ladder of life, has its own individual logos. The divine-spiritual entity behind the sun is the solar logos of our solar system. Small or great as every solar system may be, each has its own logos, the source or fountainhead of almost innumerable logoi of less degree in that system. Every man has his own spiritual logos; every atom has its own logos; every atom likewise has its own paramātman and mūlaprakṛiti, for every entity everywhere has its own highest. These things and the words which express them are obviously relative.

One meaning of the Greek *logos* is "word" — a phrase or symbol taken from the ancient Mysteries meaning the "lost word," the "lost" logos of man's heart and brain. The logos of our own planetary chain, so far as this fourth round is concerned, is the Wondrous Being or Silent Watcher (q.v.).

The term, therefore, is a relative and not an absolute one, and has many applications.

Loka (Sanskrit) A word meaning "place" or "locality" or, as much more frequently used in theosophy, a "world" or "sphere" or "plane."

The lokas are divided into rūpa-lokas and arūpa-lokas — "material worlds" and "spiritual spheres." There is a wide range of teaching connected with the lokas and talas which belongs to the deeper reaches of the esoteric philosophy. (*See also* Arūpa, Rūpa, Tala)

Lost Soul *See* Eighth Sphere, Soulless Beings

Lower Quaternary *See* Higher Triad

Luminous Arc *See* Ascending Arc

Lunar Pitṛi(s) *Lunar* of course means "belonging to the moon," while *pitṛi* is a Sanskrit word meaning "father." It is a term used in theosophy to signify the seven or ten grades of evolving entities which at the end of the lunar manvantara pass into a nirvāṇic state, to leave it aeons later as the seven or tenfold hierarchy of beings which inform the planetary chain of earth. In a general sense lunar pitṛis means all entities which originally came from the moon-chain to the earth-chain; but in a more particular and restricted sense it refers to those elements of the human constitution beneath the evolutionary standing of the agnishvāttas.

Another term for lunar pitṛis is lunar ancestors or barhishads. These lunar ancestors are usually given as of seven classes, three being arūpa, incorporeal, and four being rūpa or corporeal. There is a vast body of teaching connected with the lunar pitṛis, of which the best modern exposition thus far given is to be found in H. P. Blavatsky's *The Secret Doctrine.* Briefly, the earth-chain including our own globe Terra was populated from the moon-chain, because all entities now on earth, whatever their grade in evolution, came from the chain of the moon. (*See also* PITṚIS, AGNISHVĀTTAS)

— M —

Macrocosm The anglicized form of a Greek compound meaning "great arrangement," or more simply the great ordered system of the celestial bodies of all kinds and their various inhabitants, including the all-important idea that this arrangement is the result of interior orderly processes, the effects of indwelling consciousnesses. In other and more modern phrasing the macrocosm is the vast universe, without definable limits, which surrounds us, and with particular emphasis laid on the interior, invisible, and ethereal planes. In the visioning or view of the ancients the macrocosm was an animate kosmic entity, an "animal" in the Latin sense of this word, as an organism possessing a directing and guiding soul. But this was only the outward or exoteric view. In the Mystery schools of the archaic ages, the macrocosm was considered to be not only what is hereinbefore just stated, but also to consist more definitely and specifically of seven, ten, and even twelve planes or degrees of consciousness-substance ranging from the superdivine through all the intermediate stages to the physical, and even to degrees below the physical, these comprised in one kosmic organic unit, or what moderns would call a universe. In this sense of the word macrocosm is but another name for kosmic hierarchy (q.v.), and it must be remembered in this connection that these hierarchies are simply countless in number and not only fill but actually compose and *are* indeed the spaces of frontierless SPACE.

The macrocosm was considered to be filled full not only with gods, but with innumerable multitudes or armies of evolving entities, from the fully self-conscious to the quasi-self-conscious downwards through the merely conscious to the "unconscious." Note well that in strict usage the term macrocosm was never applied to the Boundless, to boundless, frontierless infinitude, what the Qabbalists called Eyn-sōph. In the archaic wisdom, the macrocosm, belonging in the astral world, considered in its causal aspect, was virtually interchangeable with what modern theosophists call the Absolute (q.v.).

Mahat (Sanskrit) This word means "great." Mahat is a technical term in the Brahmanic system, and is the "father-mother" of manas; it is the "mother" of the mānasaputras or sons of mind, or that element from which they spring, that element which they breathe and of which they are the children. In the Sānkhya philosophy — one of the six *darśanas* or "visions," i.e., systems of philosophical visioning of ancient India — mahat is a term that corresponds to kosmic buddhi, but more accurately perhaps to mahā-buddhi.

Mahātma (*Mahātman,* Sanskrit) "Great soul" or "great self" is the meaning of this compound word *(mahā,* "great"; *ātman,* "self"). The mahātmas are perfected men, relatively speaking, known in theosophical literature as teachers, elder brothers, masters, sages, seers, and by other names. They are indeed the "elder brothers" of mankind. They are men, not spirits — men who have evolved through self-devised efforts in individual evolution, always advancing forwards and upwards until they have now attained the lofty spiritual and intellectual human supremacy that now they hold. They were not so created by any extra-cosmic Deity, but they are men who have become what they are by means of inward spiritual striving, by spiritual and intellectual yearning, by aspiration to be greater and better, nobler and higher, just as every good man in his own way so aspires. They are farther advanced along the path of evolution than the majority of men are. They possess knowledge of nature's secret processes, and of hid mysteries, which to the average man may seem to be little short of the marvelous — yet, after all, this mere fact is of relatively small importance in comparison with the far greater and more profoundly moving aspects of their nature and lifework.

Especially are they called teachers because they are occupied in the noble duty of instructing mankind, in inspiring elevating thoughts, and in instilling impulses of forgetfulness of self into the hearts of men. Also are they sometimes called the guardians, because they are, in very truth, the guardians of the race and of the records — natural, racial, national — of past ages, portions of which they give out from time to time as fragments of a now long-forgotten wisdom, when the world is ready to listen to them; and they do this in order to advance the cause of truth and of genuine civilization founded on wisdom and brotherhood.

Never — such is the teaching — since the human race first attained self-consciousness has this order or association or society or brotherhood of exalted men been without its representatives on our earth.

It was the mahātmas who founded the modern Theosophical Society through their envoy or messenger, H. P. Blavatsky, in New York in 1875.

Man Man is in his essence a spark of the central kosmic spiritual fire. Man being an inseparable part of the universe of which he is the child — the organism of graded consciousness and substance which the human constitution contains or rather is — is a copy of the graded organism of consciousnesses and substances of the universe in its various planes of being, inner and outer, especially inner as being by far the more important and larger, because causal.

Human beings are one class of "young gods" incarnated in bodies of flesh at the present stage of their own particular evolutionary journey. The human stage of evolution is about halfway between the undeveloped life-atom and the fully developed kosmic spirit or god.

From another point of view, man is a sheaf or bundle of forces or energies. Force and matter, or spirit and substance being fundamentally one, hence, man is de facto a sheaf or bundle of matters of various and differing grades of ethereality, or of substantiality; and so are all other entities and things everywhere.

Man's nature, and the nature of the universe likewise, of which man is a reflection or microcosm or "little world," is composite of seven stages or grades or degrees of ethereality or of substantiality; or, kosmically speaking, of three generally inclusive degrees: gods, monads, and atoms. And so far as man is concerned, we may take the New Testament division of the Christians, which gives the same triform conception of man, that he is composed of spirit, soul, body — remembering, however, that all these three words are generalizing terms.

Man stands at the midway point of the evolutionary ladder of life: below him are the hosts of beings less than he is; above him are other hosts greater than he is only because older in experience, riper in wisdom, stronger in spiritual and in intellectual fiber and power. And these beings are such as they are because of the evolutionary unfoldment of the inherent faculties and powers immanent in the individuality of the inner god — the ever-living, inner, individualized spirit.

Man, then, like everything else — entity or what is called "thing" — is, to use the modern terminology of philosophical scientists, an "event," that is to say, the expression of a central consciousness-center or monad passing through one or another particular phase of its long, long pilgrimage over and through infinity, and through eternity. This, therefore, is the reason why the theosophist often speaks of the monadic consciousness-center as the pilgrim of eternity.

Man can be considered as a being composed of three essential upādhis or bases: first, the monadic or divine-spiritual; second, that which is supplied by the Lords of Light, the so-called mānasa-dhyānīs, meaning the intellectual and intuitive side of man, the element-principle that makes man *Man*; and the third upādhi we may call the vital-astral-physical.

These three bases spring from three different lines of evolution, from three different and separate hierarchies of being. This is the reason why man is composite. He is not one sole and unmixed entity; he is a composite entity, a "thing" built up of various elements, and hence his principles are to a certain extent separable. Any one of these three bases can be temporarily separated from the two others without bringing about the death of the man physically. But the elements that go to form any one of these bases cannot be separated without bringing about physical dissolution or inner dissolution.

These three lines of evolution, these three aspects or qualities of man, come from three different hierarchies or states, often spoken of as three different planes of being. The lowest comes from the vital-astral-physical earth, ultimately from the moon, our cosmogonic mother. The middle, the mānasic or intellectual-intuitional, from the sun. The monadic from the monad of monads, the supreme flower or acme, or rather the supreme seed of the universal hierarchy which forms our kosmical universe or universal kosmos.

Manas (Sanskrit) The root of this word means "to think," "to cogitate," "to reflect" — mental activity, in short. The center of the ego-consciousness in man and in any other quasi-self-conscious entity. The third substance-principle, counting downwards, of which man's constitution is composed.

Manas springs forth from buddhi (the second principle) as the fruit from the flower; but manas itself is mortal, goes to pieces at death — insofar as its lower parts are concerned. All of it that lives after death is only what is spiritual in it and that can be squeezed out of it, so to say — the "aroma" of the manas; somewhat as the chemist takes from the rose the attar or essence of roses. The monad or ātma-buddhi thereupon takes that "all" with it into the devachan, after the second death has taken place. Ātman, with buddhi and with the higher part of manas, becomes thereupon the spiritual monad of man. Strictly speaking, this is the divine monad within its vehicle — ātman and buddhi — combined with the human ego in its higher mānasic element; but they are joined into one after death, and are hence spoken of as the spiritual monad.

The three principles forming the upper triad exist each on its own plane in consciousness and power; and as human beings we continuously feel their influence despite the enshrouding veils of a psychical and astral-physical character. We know of each principle only what we have so far evolved forth of it. All we know, for instance, of the third principle (counting from the top), the manas, is what we have so far assimilated of it in this fourth round. The manas will not be fully developed in us until the end of the next round. What we now call our manas is a generalizing term for the reincarnating ego, the higher manas.

Mānasaputra(s) (Sanskrit) This is a compound word: *manas,* "mind," *putra,* "son" — "sons of mind." The teaching is that there exists a Hierarchy of Compassion, which H. P. Blavatsky sometimes called the Hierarchy of Mercy or of Pity. This is the light side of nature as contrasted with its matter side or shadow side, its night side. It is from this Hierarchy of Compassion that came those semi-divine entities at about the middle period of the third root-race of this round, who incarnated in the semi-conscious, quasi-senseless men of that period. These advanced entities are otherwise known as the solar lhas as the Tibetans call them, the solar spirits, who were the men of a former kalpa, and who during the third root-race thus sacrificed themselves in order to give us intellectual light — incarnating in those senseless psychophysical shells in order to awaken the divine flame of egoity and *self*-consciousness in the sleeping egos which we then were. They are ourselves because belonging to the same spirit-ray that we do; yet we, more strictly speaking, were those half-unconscious, half-awakened egos whom they touched with the divine fire of their own being. This, our "awakening," was called by H. P. Blavatsky, the incarnation of the mānasaputras, or the sons of mind or light. Had that incarnation not taken place, we indeed should have continued our evolution by merely "natural" causes, but it would have been slow almost beyond comprehension, almost interminable; but that act of self-sacrifice, through their immense pity, their immense love, though, indeed, acting under karmic impulse, awakened the divine fire in our own selves, gave us light and comprehension and understanding. From that time we ourselves became "sons of the gods," the faculty of self-consciousness in us was awakened, our eyes were opened, responsibility became ours; and our feet were set then definitely upon the path, that inner path, quiet, wonderful, leading us inwards back to our spiritual home.

The mānasaputras are our higher natures and, paradoxical as it is, are more largely evolved beings than we are. They were the spiritual entities who "quickened" our personal egos, which were thus evolved into self-consciousness, relatively small though that yet be. One, and yet many! As you can light an infinite number of candles from one lighted candle, so from a spark of consciousness can you quicken and enliven innumerable other consciousnesses, lying, so to speak, in sleep or latent in the life-atoms.

These mānasaputras, children of mahat, are said to have quickened and enlightened in us the manas-manas of our manas septenary, because they themselves are typically mānasic in their essential characteristic or svabhāva. Their own essential or mānasic vibrations, so to say, could cause that essence of manas in ourselves to vibrate in sympathy, much as the sounding of a musical note will cause sympathetic response in something like it, a similar note in other things. (*See also* AGNISHVĀTTAS)

Manifestation A generalizing term signifying not only the beginning but the continuance of organized kosmic activity, the latter including the various minor activities within itself. First there is of course always the Boundless in all its infinite planes and worlds or spheres, aggregatively symbolized by the ○ (or circle); then parabrahman, or the kosmic life-consciousness activity, and mūlaprakṛiti its other pole, signifying root-nature especially in its substantial aspects. Then the next stage lower, Brahman and its veil pradhāna; then Brahmā-prakṛiti or Purusha-prakṛiti (prakṛiti being also māyā); the manifested universe appearing through and by this last, Brahmā-prakṛiti, "father-mother." In other words, the second Logos or father-mother is the producing cause of manifestation through their son which, in a planetary chain, is the primordial or the originating manu, called Svāyambhuva.

When manifestation opens, prakṛiti becomes or rather is māyā; and Brahmā, the father, is the spirit of the consciousness, or the individuality. These two, Brahmā and prakṛiti, are really one, yet they are also the two aspects of the one life-ray acting and reacting upon itself, much as a man himself can say, "I am *I*." He has the faculty of self-analysis or self-division. All of us know it, we can feel it in ourselves — one side of us, in our thoughts, can be called the prakṛiti or the material element, or the māyāvi element, or the element of illusion; and the other is the spirit, the individuality, the god within.

The student should note carefully that *manifestation* is but a generalizing term, comprehensive therefore of a vast number of different and differing kinds of evolving planes or realms. For instance, there is manifestation on the divine plane; there is manifestation also on the spiritual plane; and similarly so on all the descending stages of the ladder or stair of life. There are universes whose "physical" plane is utterly invisible to us, so high is it; and there are other universes in the contrary direction, so far beneath our present physical plane that their ethereal ranges of manifestation are likewise invisible to us.

Manu Manu in the esoteric system is the entities collectively which appear first at the beginning of manifestation, and from which, like a cosmic tree, everything is derived or born. Manu actually is the spiritual tree of life of any planetary chain of manifested being. Manu is thus in one sense the third Logos; as the second is the father-mother, the Brahmā and prakṛiti; and the first is what we call the unmanifest Logos, or Brahman (neuter) and its cosmic veil pradhāna.

In other words, the second Logos, father-mother, is the producing cause of manifestation through their son, which in a planetary chain is Manu, the first of the manus being called in the archaic Hindu system Svāyambhuva.

During a Day of Brahmā or period of seven rounds, fourteen subordinate or inferior manus appear as patrons and guardians of the race cycles or life-waves (*See also* H. P. Blavatsky, *The Secret Doctrine, passim*; also MANVANTARA).

Manu is likewise the name of a great ancient Indian legislator, the alleged author of the *Laws of Manu* (*Mānava-dharma-śāstra*).

Manvantara (Sanskrit) This word is a compound, and means nothing more than "between two manus"; more literally, "manu-within or -between." A manu, as said, is the entities collectively which appear first at the beginning of manifestation; the spiritual tree of life of any planetary chain of manifested being. The second verbal element of "manvantara," or *antara,* is a prepositional suffix signifying "within" or "between"; hence the compound paraphrased means "within a manu," or "between manus." A manvantara is the period of activity between any two manus, on any plane, since in any such period there is a root-manu at the beginning of evolution, and a seed-manu at its close, preceding a pralaya (q.v.).

There are many kinds of manvantaras: *prākṛitika* manvantara — universal manvantara; *saurya* manvantara — the manvantara of the solar system; *bhaumika* manvantara — the terrestrial manvantara, or manvantara of earth; *paurusha* manvantara — the manvantara, or period of activity, of man.

A round-manvantara is the time required for one round: that is, the cycle from globe A to the last globe of the seven, and starting from the root-manu or collective "humanity" of globe A and ending with the seed-manu or collective "humanity" of Globe G.

A planetary manvantara — also called a mahā-manvantara or a kalpa — is the period of the lifetime of a planet during its seven rounds. It is also called a Day of Brahmā (q.v.), and its length is 4,320,000,000 years.

Master(s) A master is one who has his higher principles awakened and lives in them; and ordinary men do not. From the scientific standpoint, that is all there is to it; from the philosophic standpoint, we may say that a master has become, as far as he can be, more at one with the universal life; and from the religious standpoint or the spiritual standpoint, we may say that a master has developed an individual consciousness or recognition of his oneness with the Boundless. (*See also* Mahatmas)

Matter What men call matter or substance is the existent but illusory aggregate of veils surrounding the fundamental essence of the universe which is consciousness-life-substance. From another point of view, matter or substance is in one sense the most evolved form of expression of *manifested* spirit in any particular hierarchy. This is but another way of saying that matter is but inherent energies or powers or faculties of kosmical beings, unfolded, rolled out, and self-expressed. It is the nether and lowest pole of what the original and originating spirit is; for spirit is the primal or original pole of the evolutionary activity which brought forth through its own inherent energies the appearance or manifestation in the kosmic spaces of the vast aggregate of hierarchies. Between the originant or spirit and the resultant or matter, there is all the vast range of hierarchical stages or steps, thus forming the ladder of life or the ladder of being of any one such hierarchy.

When theosophists speak of spirit and substance, of which latter, matter and energy or force are the physicalized expressions, we must remember that all these terms are abstractions — generalized expressions for hosts of entities manifesting aggregatively. The whole process of evolution is the raising of units of essential matter, life-atoms (q.v.), into becoming at one with their spiritual and inmost essence. As the kosmic aeons slowly drop one after the other into the ocean of the past, matter *pari passu* is resolved back into the brilliant realms of spirit from which it originally came forth. All the sheaths of consciousness, all the blinding veils around it, arise from the matter side or dark side or night side of nature, which is matter — the nether pole of spirit.

Māyā (Sanskrit) The word comes from the root *mā,* meaning "to measure," and by a figure of speech it also comes to mean "to effect," "to form," and hence "to limit." There is an English word *mete,* meaning "to measure out," from the same Indo-European root. It is found in the Anglo-Saxon as the root *met,* in the Greek as *med,* and it is found in the Latin also in the same form.

Ages ago in the wonderful Brahmanical philosophy māyā was understood very differently from what it is now usually understood to be. As a technical term, māyā has come to mean the fabrication by man's mind of ideas derived from interior and exterior impressions, hence the *illusory* aspect of man's thoughts as he considers and tries to interpret and understand life and his surroundings; and thence was derived the sense which it technically bears, "illusion." It does *not* mean that the exterior world is nonexistent; if it were, it obviously could not be illusory. It *exists,* but *is* not. It is "measured out" or is "limited," or it stands out to the human spirit as a mirage. In other words, we do not see clearly and plainly and *in their reality* the vision and the visions which our mind and senses present to the inner life and eye.

The familiar illustrations of māyā in the Vedānta, which is the highest form that the Brahmanical teachings have taken and which is so near to our own teaching in many respects, were such as follows: A man at eventide sees a coiled rope on the ground, and springs aside, thinking it a serpent. The rope is there, but no serpent. The second illustration is what is called the "horns of the hare." The animal called the hare has no horns, but when it also is seen at eventide, its long ears seem to project from its head in such fashion that it appears even to the seeing eye as being a creature with horns. The hare has no horns, but there is then in the mind an illusory belief that an animal with horns exists there.

That is what māyā means: not that a thing seen does not exist, but that we are blinded and our mind perverted by our own thoughts and our own imperfections, and do not as yet arrive at the *real* interpretation and meaning of the world or of the universe around us. By ascending inwardly, by rising up, by inner aspiration, by an elevation of soul, we can reach upwards or rather *inwards* towards that plane where truth abides in fullness.

H. P. Blavatsky says on page 631 of the first volume of *The Secret Doctrine*:

> Esoteric philosophy, teaching an *objective* Idealism — though it regards the objective Universe and all in it as *Maya,* temporary illusion — draws a practical distinction between collective illusion, *Mahamaya,* from the purely metaphysical standpoint, and the objective relations in it between various conscious *Egos* so long as this illusion lasts.

The teaching is that māyā is thus called from the action of mūlaprakṛiti or *root*-nature, the coordinate principle of that other line of coactive consciousness which we call parabrahman. From the moment when manifestation begins, it acts dualistically, that is to say that everything in nature from that point onwards is crossed by pairs of opposites, such as long and short, high and low, night and day, good and evil, consciousness and nonconsciousness, etc., and that all these things are essentially māyic or illusory — real while they last, but the lasting is not eternal. It is through and by these pairs of opposites that the self-conscious soul learns truth. It might be said, in conclusion, that another and very convenient way of considering māyā is to understand it to mean "limitation," "restriction," and therefore imperfect cognition and recognition of reality. The imperfect mind does not see perfect truth. It labors under an illusion corresponding with its own imperfections, under a māyā, a limitation. Magical practices are frequently called māyā in the ancient Hindu books.

Māyāvi-Rūpa (Sanskrit) This is a compound of two words: *māyāvi,* the adjectival form of the word *māyā,* hence "illusory"; *rūpa,* "form"; the māyāvi-rūpa or thought-body, or illusory-body, a higher astral-mental form. The māyāvi can assume all forms or any form, at the will of an Adept. A synonymous philosophical term is protean soul. In Germany medieval mystics called it the *doppelgänger.* There is a very mystical fact connected with the māyāvi-rūpa: the Adept is enabled to project his consciousness in the māyāvi-rūpa to what would seem to the uninitiated incredible distances, while the physical body is left, as it were, intranced. In Tibet this power of projecting the māyāvi-rūpa is called hpho-wa.

Mediator *See* MEDIUM

Medium A word of curiously ill-defined significance, and used mostly if not exclusively by modern Spiritists. The general sense of the word would seem to be a person of unstable psychical temperament, or constitution rather, who is supposed to act as a canal or channel of transmission, hence "medium," between human beings and the so-called spirits.

A medium actually in the theosophical teaching is one whose inner constitution is in unstable balance, or perhaps even dislocated, so that at different times the sheaths of the inner parts of the medium's constitution function irregularly and in magnetic sympathy with currents and entities in the astral light (q.v.), more particularly in kāma-loka (q.v.). It is an exceedingly unfortunate and dangerous condition to be in, despite what the Spiritists claim for it.

Very different indeed from the medium is the *mediator,* a human being of relatively highly evolved spiritual and intellectual and psychical nature who serves as an intermediary or mediator between the members of the Great Brotherhood, the mahātmas, and ordinary humanity. There are also mediators of a still more lofty type who serve as channels of transmission for the passing down of divine and spiritual and highly intellectual powers to this sphere. Actually, every mahātma is such a mediator of this higher type, and so in even larger degree are the buddhas and the avatāras. A mediator is one of highly evolved constitution, every portion of which is under the instant and direct control of the spiritual dominating will and the loftiest intelligence which the mediator is capable of exercising. Every human being should strive to be a mediator of this kind between his own inner god and his mere brain-mind. The more he succeeds, the grander he is as a man.

Mediator, therefore, and medium are the polar antitheses of each other. The medium is irregular, negative, often irresponsible or quasi-irresponsible, and uncertain, and is not infrequently the victim or plaything of evil and degenerate entities whom theosophists call elementaries, having their habitat in the astral light of the earth; whereas the mediator is one more or less fully insouled or inspirited with divine, spiritual, and intellectual powers and their corresponding faculties and organs.

Mesmerism An ill-understood branch of human knowledge, developed within fairly recent times, connected with the existence of the psychomagnetic fluid in man which can be employed by the will for purposes either good or evil. It has been called animal magnetism, but more often in former times than at present. The first European who rediscovered and openly proclaimed the existence of this subtle psychomagnetic fluid in man was Dr. Friedrich Anton Mesmer, born in Germany in 1733, who died in 1815. His honesty and his theories have been more or less vindicated in modern times by later students of the subject.

There are distinct differences as among mesmerism, hypnotism, psychologization, and suggestion, etc. (*See also* Hypnotism)

Messenger In the theosophical sense, an individual who comes with a mandate from the Lodge of the Masters of Wisdom and Compassion to do a certain work in the world.

Only real genius — indeed something more than merely human genius — only extraordinary spiritual and intellectual capacity, native to the constitution of some lofty human being, could explain the reason for the choice of such messengers. But, indeed, this is not saying enough; because in addition to genius and to merely native spiritual and intellectual capacity such a messenger must possess through initiatory training the capacity of throwing at will the intermediate or psychological nature into a state of perfect quiescence or receptivity for the stream of divine-spiritual inspiration flowing forth from the messenger's own inner divinity or monadic essence. It is obvious, therefore, that such a combination of rare and unusual qualities is not often found in human beings; and, when found, such a one is fit for the work to be done by such a messenger of the Association of great ones.

The Masters of Wisdom and Compassion and Peace send their envoys continuously into the world of men, one after the other, and in consequence these envoys are working in the world among men all the time. Happy are they whose hearts recognize the footfalls of those crossing the mountaintops of the Mystic East. The messengers do not always do public work before the world, but frequently work in the silences and unknown of men, or relatively unknown. At certain times, however, they are commissioned and empowered and directed to do their work publicly and to make public announcement of their mission. Such, for instance, was the case of H. P. Blavatsky.

Metempsychosis (Greek) A compound vocable which may be rendered briefly by "insouling after insouling," or "changing soul after soul." Metempsychosis contains the specific meaning that the soul of an entity, human or other, moves not merely from condition to condition, migrates not merely from state to state or from body to body; but also that it is an indivisible entity in its inmost essence, which is pursuing a course along its own particular evolutionary path as an individual monad, taking upon itself soul after soul; and it is the adventures which befall the soul, in assuming soul after soul, which in their aggregate are grouped together under this word metempsychosis.

In ordinary language metempsychosis is supposed to be a synonym for transmigration, reincarnation, preexistence, and palingenesis, etc., but all these words in the esoteric philosophy have specific meanings of their own, and should not be confused. It is of course evident that these words have strict relations with each other, as, for instance, every soul in its metempsychosis also transmigrates in its own particular sense; and inversely every transmigrating entity also has its metempsychosis or soul-changings in its own particular sense. But these connections or interminglings of meanings must not be confused with the specific significance attached to each one of these words.

The essential meaning of metempsychosis can perhaps be briefly described by saying that a monad during the course of its evolutionary peregrinations throws forth from itself periodically a new soul-garment or soul-sheath, and this changing of souls or soul-sheaths as the ages pass is called metempsychosis. (*See also* Transmigration, Reincarnation, Preexistence, Palingenesis)

Metensomatosis (Greek) A compound word of which the significance may perhaps be briefly rendered thus: "changing body after body." The reference is to a reimbodying entity which does not necessarily use human bodies of flesh only, in which respect this word differs from reincarnation (q.v.), but bodies of appropriate yet different physical material concordant with the evolutionary stage which the human race may have reached at any time, and with the plane or sphere of nature on which the reimbodiment takes place. This word, because of the intricate ideas involved, is very difficult to explain properly or even to hint at in a few words, but perhaps it may be made more clear by the following observation: In far past ages the human race had bodies, but not bodies of flesh; and in far distant ages of the future, the human race will likewise have bodies, but not necessarily bodies of flesh. Actually, our teaching in this respect is that in those far-distant periods of the future, human bodies of that time will be compact of ether or, what comes to much the same thing, of luminous matter which may very properly be called concreted light.

Microcosm (Greek) A compound meaning "little arrangement," "little world," a term applied by ancient and modern mystics to man when considering the seven, ten, and even twelve aspects or phases or organic parts of his constitution, from the superdivine down to and even below the physical body.

Just as throughout the macrocosm (q.v.) there runs one law, one fundamental consciousness, one essential orderly arrangement and habitude to which everything contained within the encompassing macrocosm of necessity conforms, just so does every such contained entity or thing, because it is an inseparable part of the macrocosm, contain in itself, evolved or unevolved, implicit or explicit, active or latent, everything that the macrocosm contains — whether energy, power, substance, matter, faculty, or what not. The microcosm, therefore, considered as man or indeed any other organic entity, is correctly viewed as a reflection or copy in miniature of the great macrocosm, the former being contained, with hosts of others like it, within the encircling frontiers of the macrocosm. Thus it was stated by the ancient mystics that the destiny of man, the microcosm, is coeval with the universe or macrocosm. Their origin is the same, their energies and substances are the same, and their future is the same, of course *mutatis mutandis.* It was no vain figment of imagination and no idle figure of speech which brought the ancient mystics to declare man to be a son of the Boundless.

The teaching is one of the most suggestive and beautiful in the entire range of the esoteric philosophy, and the deductions that the intuitive student will immediately draw from this teaching themselves become keys opening even larger portals of understanding. The universe, the macrocosm, is thus seen to be the home of the microcosm or man, in the former of which the latter is at home everywhere.

Milky Way, The The Milky Way or galaxy is held to be our own especial home-universe. The nebulae are in many cases taken to be what are called island-universes, that is to say, vast aggregations of stars, many numbers of them with their respective planets around them, and all gathered together in these individual world-clusters. Of course there are nebulae of other kinds, but to these reference is not here made. Of the island-universes, there are doubtless hundreds of thousands of them; but as none of these has as yet [1933] been discovered to be as large in diameter, or as thick through, as is our own Milky Way system — which system has somewhat the shape of a lens or of a thin watch — the astronomers call our Milky Way by the popular name of continent-universe; and such other nebular star-clusters which we see and which are in many cases really vast masses of millions or billions of suns, are called island-universes.

Our own Milky Way, could it be seen from some vast kosmic distance, would doubtless appear as a nebula or large star-cluster; and to certain percipient watchers our galaxy might even probably appear to be a spiral nebula, or perhaps an annular nebula. Our own sun is one of the stars in the cluster of the Milky Way, and is said by astronomers to be situated some distance, kosmically speaking, from the central portion of our Milky Way system, and a trifle to the north of the plane passing through the figure-center of the galaxy.

The Milky Way is not only a vast star-cluster of suns in all-various degrees of evolutionary growth, but it is also the storehouse of celestial bodies-to-be. In this last respect, it is, as it were, the kosmic nursery from which seeds of future suns go forth to begin their manvantaric evolutionary courses. There are vast and fascinating mysteries connected with the Milky Way even in matters that concern the destiny of us human beings, as well as of all other entities of our solar system. The profound teachings which theosophy hints at under the topics of circulations of the kosmos (q.v.) and peregrinations of the monads are directly connected with the doctrines just referred to. The whole matter, however, is of so recondite a character that it is impossible here to do more than point suggestively to it.

Moksha (Sanskrit) This word comes from *moksh,* meaning "to release," "to set free," and is probably a desiderative of the root *much,* from which the word *mukti* also comes. The meaning of this word is that when a spirit, a monad, or a *spiritual radical,* has so grown in evolution that it has first become a man, and is set free interiorly, inwardly, and from a man has become a planetary spirit or dhyān-chohan or lord of meditation, and has gone still higher, to become *interiorly* a Brahman, and from a Brahman the Parabrahman for its hierarchy, then it is absolutely perfected, relatively speaking, *free, released* — perfected for that great period of time which to us seems almost an eternity so long is it, virtually incomputable by the human intellect. Now this also is the real meaning of the much abused word Absolute (q.v.), limited in comparison with things still more immense, still more sublime; but so far as we can think of it, released or freed from the chains or bonds of material existence. One who is thus released or freed is called a jīvanmukta (q.v.). (*See also* NIRVĀṆA)

Monad A spiritual entity which to us humans is indivisible; it is a divine-spiritual life-atom, but indivisible because its essential characteristic, *as we humans conceive it,* is homogeneity; while that of the physical atom, above which our consciousness soars, is divisible, is a composite heterogeneous particle.

Monads are eternal, unitary, individual life-centers, consciousness-centers, deathless during any solar manvantara, therefore ageless, unborn, undying. Consequently, each one such — and their number is infinite — is the center of the All, for the divine or the All is THAT which has its center everywhere, and its circumference or limiting boundary nowhere.

Monads are spiritual-substantial entities, self-motivated, self-impelled, self-conscious, in infinitely varying degrees, the ultimate elements of the universe. These monads engender other monads as one seed will produce multitudes of other seeds; so up from each such monad springs a host of living entities in the course of illimitable time, each such monad being the fountainhead or parent, in which all others are involved, and from which they spring.

Every monad is a seed, wherein the sum total of powers appertaining to its divine origin are latent, that is to say unmanifested; and evolution consists in the growth and development of all these seeds or children monads, whereby the universal life expresses itself in innumerable beings.

As the monad descends into matter, or rather as its ray — one of other innumerable rays proceeding from it — is propelled into matter, it secretes from itself and then excretes on each one of the seven planes through which it passes, its various vehicles, all overshadowed by the self, the same self in you and in me, in plants and in animals, in fact in all that is and belongs to that hierarchy. This is the one self, the supreme self or paramātman of the hierarchy. It illumines and follows each individual monad and all the latter's hosts of rays — or children monads. Each such monad is a spiritual seed from the previous manvantara, which manifests as a monad in this manvantara; and this monad through its rays throws out from itself by secretion and then excretion all its vehicles. These vehicles are, first, the spiritual ego, the reflection or copy in miniature of the monad itself, but *individualized* through the manvantaric evolution, "bearing" or "carrying" as a vehicle the monadic ray. The latter cannot directly contact the lower planes, because it is of the monadic essence itself, the latter *a still higher ray* of the infinite Boundless composed of infinite multiplicity in unity. (*See also* INDIVIDUALITY)

Morals, Morality What is the basis of morals? This is the most important question that can be asked of any system of thought. Is morality based on the dicta of man? Is morality based on the conviction in most men's hearts that for human safety it is necessary to have certain abstract rules which it is merely *convenient* to follow? Are we mere opportunists? Or is morality, ethics, based on truth, which it is not merely expedient for man to follow, but necessary? Surely upon the latter! Morals is right conduct based upon right views, right thinking.

In the third fundamental postulate of *The Secret Doctrine* [1:17] we find the very elements, the very fundamentals, of a system of morality greater than which, profounder than which, more persuasive than which, perhaps, it would be impossible to imagine anything.

On what, then, is morality based? And by morality is not meant merely the opinion which some pseudo-philosophers have, that morality is more or less that which is "good for the community," based on the mere meaning of the Latin word *mores,* "good customs," as opposed to bad. No! Morality is that instinctive hunger of the human heart to do righteousness, to do good to every man because it is good and satisfying and ennobling to do so.

When man realizes that he is one with all that is, inwards and outwards, high and low; that he is one with all, not merely as members of a community are one, not merely as individuals of an army are one, but like the molecules of our own flesh, like the atoms of the molecule, like the electrons of the atom, composing one unity — not a mere union but a spiritual *unity* — then he sees truth. (*See also* ETHICS)

Mudrā (Sanskrit) A general name for certain intertwinings or positions of the fingers of the two hands, used alone or together, in devotional yoga or exoteric religious worship, and these mudrās or digital positions are held by many Oriental mystics to have particular esoteric significance. They are found both in the Buddhist statues of northern Asia, especially those belonging to the Yogāchāra school, and also in India where they are perhaps particularly affected by the Hindu tāntrikas. There is doubtless a good deal of hid efficacy in holding the fingers in proper position during meditation, but to the genuine occult student the *symbolic* meaning of such mudrās or digital positions is by far more useful and interesting. The subject is too intricate, and of importance too small, to call for much detail of explanation here, or even to attempt a full exposition of the subject.

Mukti *See* Moksha

Mūlaprakṛiti (Sanskrit) A compound containing *mūla,* "root," *prakṛiti,* "nature," root-matter or root-nature. Corresponding to it as the other or active pole is parabrahman, from which Brahman (neuter), the first or unmanifest Logos, proceeds. Mūlaprakṛiti, therefore, as the kosmic veil of parabrahman, may be called homogeneous or undifferentiated primordial substance. It is the fountain or root of ākāśa (q.v.). (*See also* Prakṛiti)

Music of the Spheres Every sphere that runs its course in the abysmal depths of space sings a song as it passes along. Every little atom is attuned to a musical note. It is in constant movement, in constant vibration at speeds which are incomprehensible to the ordinary brain-mind of man; and each such speed has its own numerical quantity, in other words its own numerical note, and therefore sings that note. This is called the music of the spheres, and if man had the power of spiritual clairaudience (q.v.), the life surrounding him would be one grand sweet song: his very body would be as it were a symphonic orchestra, singing some magnificent, incomprehensible, musical symphonic composition. The growth of a flower, for instance, would be like a changing melody running along from day to day; he could hear the grass grow, and understand why it grows; he could hear the atoms sing and see their movements, and hear the unison of the songs of all individual atoms, and the melodies that any physical body produces; and he would know what the stars in their courses are constantly singing.

Mysteries The Mysteries were divided into two general parts, the Less Mysteries and the Greater.

The Less Mysteries were very largely composed of dramatic rites or ceremonies, with some teaching; the Greater Mysteries were composed of, or conducted almost entirely on the ground of, study; and the doctrines taught in them later were proved by personal experience in initiation. In the Greater Mysteries was explained, among other things, the secret meaning of the mythologies of the old religions, as, for instance, the Greek.

The active and nimble mind of the Greeks produced a mythology which for grace and beauty is perhaps without equal, but it nevertheless is very difficult to explain; the Mysteries of Samothrace and of Eleusis — the greater ones — explained among other things what these myths meant. These myths formed the basis of the *exoteric* religions; but note well that exotericism does not mean that the thing which is taught exoterically is in itself false, but merely that it is a teaching given without the key to it. Such teaching is symbolic, illusory, touching on the truth — the truth is there, but without the key to it, which is the esoteric meaning, it yields no proper sense.

We have the testimony of the Greek and Roman initiates and thinkers that the ancient Mysteries of Greece taught men, above everything else, to live rightly and to have a noble hope for the life after death. The Romans derived their Mysteries from those of Greece.

The mythological aspect comprises only a portion — and a relatively small portion — of what was taught in the Mystery schools in Greece, principally at Samothrace and at Eleusis. At Samothrace was taught the same mystery-teaching that was current elsewhere in Greece, but here it was more developed and recondite, and the foundation of these mystery-teachings was *morals* (q.v.). The noblest and greatest men of ancient times in Greece were initiates in the Mysteries of these two seats of esoteric knowledge.

In other countries farther to the east, there were other Mystery schools or "colleges," and this word college by no means necessarily meant a mere temple or building; it meant association, as in our modern word *colleague,* "associate." The Teutonic tribes of northern Europe, the Germanic tribes, which included Scandinavia, had their Mystery colleges also; and teacher and neophytes stood on the bosom of Mother Earth, under Father Ether, the boundless sky, or in subterranean receptacles, and taught and learned. The core, the heart, the center, of the teaching of the ancient Mysteries was the abstruse problems dealing with death. (*See also* GURU-PARAMPARĀ)

Mysticism A word originally derived from the Greek and having a wide range of meaning in modern Occidental religious and philosophical literature. A mystic may be said to be one who has intuitions or intimations of the existence of inner and superior worlds, and who attempts to ally himself or to come into self-conscious communion with them and the beings inhabiting these inner and invisible worlds.

The word mysticism, of course, has various shades of significance, and a large number of definitions could easily be written following the views of different mystical writers on this theme. From the theosophical or occult point of view, however, a mystic is one who has inner convictions often based on inner vision and knowledge of the existence of spiritual and ethereal universes of which our outer physical universe is but the shell; and who has some inner knowledge that these universes or worlds or planes or spheres, with their hosts of inhabitants, are intimately connected with the origin, destiny, and even present nature of the world which surrounds us.

Genuine mysticism is an ennobling study. The average mystic, however, is one who lacks the direct guidance derived from personal teaching received from a master or spiritual superior.

— N —

Nature The consciousness side of nature is composed of vast hierarchies of gods, developed cosmical spirits, spiritual entities, cosmic graduates in the university of life. The material side of nature is the heterogeneous matter, the material world in its many various planes, in all stages of imperfection — but all these stages filled with armies of entities evolving and growing. The proper term for nature in modern theosophical usage is prakṛiti or still more accurately mūlaprakṛiti — the ever-living kosmic producer, the eternally fecund mother, of the universe. When a theosophist speaks of nature, unless he limits the term to the physical world, he never means the physical world alone, but the vast reaches of universal kosmos and more particularly the inner realms, the causal factors of the boundless All. Hence, a growing understanding of nature in this sense — which is another way of saying an understanding of reality — obviously provides the only basis of a religion founded on the changeless realities.

Nirmāṇakāya (Sanskrit) A compound of two words: *nirmāṇa,* a participle meaning "forming," "creating"; *kāya,* a word meaning "body," "robe," "vehicle"; thus, *nirmāṇakāya* means "formed-body." A nirmāṇakāya, however, is really a *state* assumed by or entered into by a bodhisattva — an individual man made semi-divine who, to use popular language, instead of choosing his reward in the nirvāṇa of a less degree, remains on earth out of pity and compassion for inferior beings, clothing himself in a nirmāṇakāyic vesture. When that state is ended the nirmāṇakāya ends.

A nirmāṇakāya is a complete man possessing all the principles of his constitution except the liṅga-śarīra and its accompanying physical body. He is one who lives on the plane of being next superior to the physical plane, and his purpose in so doing is to save men from themselves by being with them, and by continuously instilling thoughts of self-sacrifice, of self-forgetfulness, of spiritual and moral beauty, of mutual help, of compassion, and of pity.

Nirmāṇakāya is the third or lowest, exoterically speaking, of what is called in Sanskrit *trikāya* or "three bodies." The highest is the *dharmakāya,* in which state are the nirvāṇīs and full pratyeka buddhas, etc.; the second state is the *sambhogakāya,* intermediate between the former and, thirdly, the *nirmāṇakāya.* The nirmāṇakāya vesture or condition enables one entering it to live in touch and sympathy with the world of men. The sambhogakāya enables one in that state to be conscious indeed to a certain extent of the world of men and its griefs and sorrows, but with little power or impulse to render aid. The dharmakāya vesture is so pure and holy, and indeed so high, that the one possessing the dharmakāya or who is in it, is virtually out of all touch with anything inferior to himself. It is, therefore, in the nirmāṇakāya vesture if not in physical form that live and work the Buddhas of Compassion, the greatest sages and seers, and all the superholy men who through striving through ages of evolution bring forth into manifestation and power and function the divinity within. The doctrine of the nirmāṇakāyas is one of the most suggestive, profound, and beautiful teachings of the esoteric philosophy. (*See also* Dharmakāya, Sambhogakāya)

Nirvāṇa (Sanskrit) This is a compound: *nir,* "out," and *vāna,* the past participle passive of the root *vā,* "to blow," literallly meaning "blown out." So badly has the significance of the ancient Indian thought (and even its language, the Sanskrit) been understood, that for many years erudite European scholars were discussing whether being "blown out" meant actual entitative annihilation or not. But the being blown out refers only to the lower principles in man.

Nirvāṇa is a very different thing from the "heavens." Nirvāṇa is a state of utter bliss and complete, untrammeled consciousness, a state of absorption in pure kosmic Being, and is the wondrous destiny of those who have reached superhuman knowledge and purity and spiritual illumination. It really is *personal-individual* absorption into or rather identification with the Self — the highest SELF. It is also the state of the monadic entities in the period that intervenes between minor manvantaras or rounds of a planetary chain; and more fully so between each seven-round period or Day of Brahmā, and the succeeding day or new kalpa of a planetary chain. At these last times, starting forth from the seventh sphere in the seventh round, the monadic entities will have progressed far beyond even the highest state of devachan. Too pure and too far advanced even for such a condition as the devachanic felicity, they go to their appropriate sphere and condition, which latter is the nirvāṇa following the end of the seventh round.

Devachan (q.v.) and nirvāṇa are not localities. They are states, states of the beings in those respective spiritual conditions. Devachan is the intermediate state; nirvāṇa is the superspiritual state; and avīchi, popularly called the lowest of the hells, is the nether pole of the spiritual condition. These three are states of beings having habitat in the lokas or talas, in the worlds of the kosmic egg.

So far as the individual human being is concerned, the nirvāṇic state or condition may be attained to by great spiritual seers and sages, such as Gautama the Buddha, and even by men less progressed than he; because in these cases of the attaining of the nirvāṇa even during a man's life on earth, the meaning is that one so attaining has through evolution progressed so far along the path that all the lower personal part of him is become thoroughly impersonalized, the personal has put on the garment of impersonality, and such a man thereafter lives in the nirvāṇic condition of the spiritual monad.

As a concluding thought, it must be pointed out that nirvāṇa, while the *ultima thule* of the perfection to be attained by any human being, nevertheless stands less high in the estimate of mystics than the condition of the bodhisattva. For the bodhisattva, although standing on the threshold of nirvāṇa and seeing and understanding its ineffable glory and peace and rest, nevertheless retains his consciousness in the worlds of men, in order to consecrate his vast faculties and powers to the service of all that is. The buddhas in their higher parts enter the nirvāṇa, in other words, assume the dharmakāya state or vesture, whereas the bodhisattva assumes the nirmāṇakāya vesture, thereafter to become an ever-active and compassionate and beneficent influence in the world. The buddha indeed may be said to act indirectly and by long distance control, thus indeed helping the world diffusively or by diffusion; but the bodhisattva acts directly and positively and with a directing will in works of compassion, both for the world and for individuals.

Nivṛitti *See* Involution; *also* Evolution

Niyama *See* Samādhi

Noetic (Greek) The adjective belonging to *nous* (q.v.).

Nous (Greek) This is a term frequently used by Plato for what in modern theosophical literature is usually called the higher manas or higher mind or spiritual soul, the union and characteristics of the buddhi-manas in man overshadowed by the ātman. The distinction to be drawn between the nous on the one hand, and the animal soul or *psyche* and its workings on the other hand, is very sharp, and the two must not be confused. In occultism the kosmic nous is the third Logos, and in the case of man's own constitution, or in human pneumatology, the nous is the buddhi-manas or higher manas or spiritual monad.

— O —

Obscuration This is a word coined by A. P. Sinnett, one of the pioneers in theosophical propaganda. A far better word than obscuration would have been *dormancy* or *sleep,* because this word obscuration actually rather obscures the sense. A man is not "obscured" when he sleeps. The inner faculties may be so, in a sense; but it is better actually to state in more appropriate words just what the real condition is. It is that of sleep, or latency — of dormancy, rather. Thus when one of the seven kingdoms has passed through its seven periods of progress, of evolution, it goes into dormancy or obscuration.

Likewise when the seven kingdoms — from the first elemental kingdom upwards to the human — have finished their evolution on globe A (for instance) during the first round, globe A then goes into obscuration, that is, into dormancy; it goes to sleep. Everything left on it is now dormant, is sleeping, awaiting the incoming, when round two begins, of the life-waves which have just left it. Again, when the life-waves have run their full sevenfold course, or their seven stock-races or root-races on globe B, then globe B in its turn goes into dormancy or obscuration, which is not *pralaya* (q.v.); and the distinction between pralaya and obscuration is an extremely important one. It may be possible in popular usage at times to call the state of dormancy by the name of pralaya in a very limited and particular sense; but pralaya really means disintegration and disappearance, like that of death. But obscuration is sleep — dormancy.

Thus is it with each one of the seven globes of the planetary chain, one after the other, each one going into obscuration when a life-wave has left it, *so far as that particular life-wave is concerned.* When the final or rather the last representatives of the last root-race of the last life-wave leave it, each globe then goes to sleep or into dormancy.

During a planetary obscuration or planetary rest period, at the end of a round, the entities leave the last globe, the seventh, and enter into a (lower) nirvāṇic period of manvantaric repose, answering to the devachanic or between-life state of the human entity between one life on earth and the next life on earth. There is one very important point of the teachings to be noted here: a globe when a life-wave leaves it does not remain in obscuration or continuously dormant until the same life-wave returns to it in the next round. The life-waves succeed each other in regular file, and each life-wave as it enters a globe has its period of beginning, its efflorescence, and its decay, and then leaves the globe in obscuration so far as that particular life-wave is concerned. But the globe within a relatively short time receives a succeeding life-wave, which runs through its courses and leaves the globe again in obscuration so far as this last life-wave is concerned, etc. It is obvious, therefore, that a period of obscuration on any globe of the planetary chain is much shorter than the term of a full planetary round.

Occultism This word meant originally only the *science of things hid*; even in the Middle Ages of Europe those philosophers who were the forerunners of the modern scientists, those who then studied physical nature, called their science occultism, and their studies occult, meaning the things that were hid or not known to the common run of mankind. Such a medieval philosopher was Albertus Magnus, a German; and so also was Roger Bacon, an Englishman — both of the thirteenth century of the Christian era.

Occultism as theosophists use the term, and as it should be used, means the study of the hid things of Being, the science of life or universal nature. In one sense this word can be used to mean the study of unusual "phenomena," which meaning it usually has today among people who do not think of the vastly larger field of *causes* which occultism, properly speaking, investigates. Doubtless mere physical phenomena have their place in study, but they are on the frontier, on the outskirts — the superficialities — of occultism. The study of true occultism means penetrating deep into the *causal* mysteries of Being.

Occultism is a generalizing term for the entire body of the occult sciences — the sciences of the secrets of universal nature; as H. P. Blavatsky phrases it, "physical and psychic, mental and spiritual; called Hermetic and Esoteric Sciences." Occultism may be considered also to be a word virtually interchangeable with the phrase esoteric philosophy, with, however, somewhat more emphasis laid on the occult or secret or hid portions of the esoteric philosophy. Genuine occultism embraces not merely the physical, physiological, psychological, and spiritual portions of man's being, but has an equal and indeed a perhaps wider range in the studies dealing with the structure and operations as well as the origin and destiny of the kosmos.

Ojas (Sanskrit) A word meaning "energy," "vigor," "power." It is often used for the principle of vital heat permeating the human constitution. From this fact, it sometimes is employed to signify virility or the generative faculty. Its use is extremely uncommon in modern occult literature.

Om A word considered very holy in the Brahmanical literature. It is a syllable of invocation, as well as of benediction and of affirmation, and its general usage (as elucidated in the literature treating of it, which is rather voluminous, for this word Om has attained almost divine reverence on the part of vast numbers of Hindus) is that it should never be uttered aloud, or in the presence of an outsider, a foreigner, or a non-initiate, and it should be uttered in the silence of one's mind, in peace of heart, and in the intimacy of one's "inner closet." There is strong reason to believe, however, that this syllable of invocation was uttered, and uttered aloud in a monotone, by the disciples in the presence of their teacher. This word is always placed at the beginning of any scripture or prayer that is considered of unusual sanctity.

It is said that by prolonging the uttering of this word, both of the *o* and the *m,* with the mouth closed, the sound re-echoes in and arouses vibration in the skull, and affects, *if the aspirations be pure,* the different nervous centers of the body for good.

The Brāhmaṇas say that it is an unholy thing to utter this word in any place which is unholy. It is sometimes written *Aum.*

Outer Round *See* Round

— P —

Palingenesis (Greek) A compound which means "coming again into being," or "becoming again." The meaning attached to this word is quite specific, although having a wide and general application. The idea included in it may be illustrated, as is found in the philosophical literature of the ancients who lived around the Mediterranean Sea, by the example of the oak which produces its seed, the acorn, the acorn in its turn producing a new oak containing the same life that was passed on to it from the mother oak — or the father oak. This transmission of an identic life in cyclical recurring phases is the specific meaning of the word palingenesis. Thus the thought is different from the respective ideas contained in the other words connected with the doctrine of reimbodiment (q.v.). Perhaps another way of stating the specific meaning would be by stating that palingenesis signifies the continuous transmission of an identic life producing at each transformation a new manifestation or result, these several results being in each case a palingenesis or "new becoming" of the same life-stream. Its specific meaning is quite different from that imbodied in the word transmigration (q.v.).

Parabrahman (Sanskrit) *Para* is a word meaning "beyond." *Brahman* (neuter) is sometimes used as the universal self or spirit; also called *paramātman* (q.v.). Beyond Brahman is the para-Brahman. Note the deep philosophical meaning of this — there is no attempt here to limit the illimitable, the ineffable, by adjectives. In the Sanskrit Vedas and in the works deriving therefrom and belonging to the Vedic literary cycle, this "beyond" is called *tat,* "THAT," as this world of manifestations is called *idam,* "This."

Parabrahman is intimately connected with mūlaprakṛiti (q.v.). Their interaction and intermingling cause the first nebulous thrilling, if the words will pass, of the universal life when spiritual desire first arose in it in the beginnings of things. Parabrahman, therefore, literally means "beyond Brahman"; and strictly speaking it is Brahman to which the Occidental term Absolute (q.v.) should be applied. Parabrahman is no entity, is no individual or individualized being. It is a convenient technical word with conveniently vague philosophical significancy, implying whatever is beyond the Absolute or Brahman of any hierarchy. Just as Brahman is the summit of a kosmic hierarchy, so, following the same line of thought, the parabrahman is "whatever is beyond Brahman."

Paramātman (Sanskrit) The "primordial self" or the "self beyond," the permanent SELF, the Brahman or universal spirit-soul. A compound term meaning the highest or universal ātman. *Parama,* "primordial," "supreme," etc.; the root of *ātman* is hardly known — its origin is uncertain, but the general meaning is that of "self." Paramātman consequently means the "supreme self," or the summit or flower of a hierarchy, the root-base or source of that kosmic self.

Selflessness is the attribute of the paramātman, the universal self, where all personality vanishes.

The universal self is the heart of the universe, for these two phrases are but two manners of expressing the same thing; it is the source of our being; it is also the goal whither we are all marching, we and the hierarchies above us as well as the hierarchies and the entities which compose them inferior to us. All come from the same ineffable source, the heart of Being, the universal self, pass at one period of their evolutionary journey through the stage of humanity, gaining thereby self-consciousness or the ego-self, the "I am I," and they find it, as they advance along this evolutionary path, expanding gradually into universal consciousness — an expansion which never has an end, because the universal consciousness is endless, limitless, boundless.

The paramātman is spiritually practically identical with what the theosophist has in mind when he speaks of the Absolute (q.v.); and consequently paramātman, though possessing a wide range of meanings, is virtually identical with Brahman. Of course when the human mind or consciousness ascends in meditation up the rungs of the endless ladder of life and realizes that the paramātman of one hierarchy or kosmos is but one of a multitude of other paramātmans of other kosmic hierarchies, the realization comes that even the vague term parabrahman (q.v.) may at certain moments of philosophical introspection be found to be the frontierless paramātman of boundless space; but in this last usage of paramātman the word obviously becomes a sheer generalizing expression for boundless life, boundless consciousness, boundless substance. This last use of the word, while correct enough, is hardly to be recommended because apt to introduce confusion, especially in Occidental minds with our extraordinary tendency to take generalizations for concrete realities.

Path, The Universal nature, our great parent, exists inseparably in each one of us, in each entity everywhere, and no separation of the part from the whole, of the individual from the kosmos, is possible in any other than a purely illusory sense. This points out to us with unerring definiteness and also directs us to the sublime path to utter reality. It is the path inwards, ever onwards within, which is endless and which leads into vast inner realms of wisdom and knowledge; for, as all the great world philosophies tell us so truly, if you *know yourself* you then know the universe, because each one of you is an inseparable part of it and it is all in you, its child.

It is obvious from this last reflection that the sole essential difference between any two grades of the evolving entities which infill and compose the kosmos is a difference of consciousness, of understanding; and this consciousness and understanding come to the evolving entity in only one way — by unwrapping or unfolding the intrinsic faculties or powers of that entity's own inner being. *This* is the path, as the mystics of all ages have put it.

The pathway is within yourself. There is no other pathway for you individually than the pathway leading ever inwards towards your own inner god. The pathway of another is the same pathway for that other; but it is not your pathway, because your pathway is your Self, as it is for that other one his Self — and yet, wonder of wonders, mystery of mysteries, the Self is the same in all. All tread the same pathway, but each man must tread it himself, and no one can tread it for another; and this pathway leads to unutterable splendor, to unutterable expansion of consciousness, to unthinkable bliss, to perfect peace.

Personality Theosophists draw a clear and sharp distinction, not of essence but of quality, between personality and individuality (q.v.). Personality comes from the Latin word *persona,* which means a mask, through which the actor, the spiritual individuality, speaks. The personality is all the lower man: all the psychical and astral and physical impulses and thoughts and tendencies, and what not. It is the reflection in matter of the individuality; but being a material thing it can lead us downwards, although it is in essence a reflection of the highest. Freeing ourselves from the domination of the person, the mask, the veil, through which the individuality acts, then we show forth all the spiritual and so-called superhuman qualities; and this will happen in the future, in the far distant aeons of the future, when every human being shall have become a buddha, a christ. Such is the destiny of the human race.

In occultism the distinction between the personality and the immortal individuality is that drawn between the lower quaternary or four lower principles of the human constitution and the three higher principles of the constitution or higher triad. The higher triad is the individuality; the personality is the lower quaternary. The combination of these two into a unity during a lifetime on earth produces what we now call the human being. The personality comprises within its range all the characteristics and memories and impulses and karmic attributes of one physical life; whereas the individuality is the aeonic ego, imperishable and deathless for the period of a solar manvantara. It is the individuality through its ray or human astral-vital monad which reincarnates time after time and thus clothes itself in one personality after another personality.

Philosophy An operation of the human spirit-mind in its endeavor to understand not merely the *how* of things, but the *why* of things — why and how things are as they are. Philosophy is one phase of a triform method of understanding the nature of nature, of universal nature, and of its multiform and multifold workings, and philosophy cannot be separated from the other two phases (science and religion), if we wish to gain a true and complete picture of things *as they are in themselves.* It is a capital mistake of Western thought to suppose that science, religion, and philosophy are three separate and unrelated operations of thought.

The idea when pondered upon is immediately seen to be ludicrously false, because all these three are but phases of operations of human consciousness. Not one of these three — philosophy, religion, or science — can be divorced from the other two, and if the attempt be made so to divorce them, the result is spiritual and intellectual dissatisfaction, and the mind senses an incompleteness. Consequently any philosophy which is unscientific and irreligious, or any religion which is unscientific and unphilosophical, and any science which is unphilosophical and unreligious, is de facto erroneous because incomplete. These three are simply three aspects or phases of a fundamental reality which is consciousness.

Philosophy is that aspect of the human consciousness which is correlative, and which seeks the bonds of union among things and exposes them, when found, as existing in the manifold and diverse forms of natural processes and the so-called laws which demonstrate their existence. (*See also* Religion, Science)

Pitṛi(s) (Sanskrit) A word meaning "father." There are seven (or ten) classes of pitṛis. They are called "fathers" because they are more particularly the actual progenitors of our lower principles; whereas the dhyāni-chohans are actually, in one most important sense, our own *selves.* We were born from them; we were the monads, we were the atoms, the souls, projected, sent forth, emanated, by the dhyānis.

The pitṛis, for easy understanding, may be divided into two great groups, the solar and lunar. The lunar pitṛis or barhishads, as the name implies, came from the moon-chain; while the solar pitṛis whom we may group under the expressive name agnishvātta-pitṛis are those dhyān-chohans which have not the physical "creative fire," because they belong to a much superior sphere of being, but they have all the fires of the spiritual-intellectual realms active or latent within them as the case may be. In preceding manvantaras they had finished their evolution so far as the realms of astral and physical matter were concerned, and when the proper time came in the cycling ages, the agnishvātta-pitṛis came to the rescue of those who had only the physical creative fire, or barhishad-pitṛis, the lunar pitṛis, inspiring and enlightening these lower pitṛis with the spiritual and intellectual energies or "fires."

In other words, the lunar pitṛis may briefly be said to be those consciousness-centers in the human constitution which feel humanly, which feel instinctually, and which possess the brain-mind mentality. The agnishvātta-pitṛis are those monadic centers of the human constitution which are of a purely spiritual type. (*See also* AGNISHVĀTTAS, LUNAR PITṚIS)

Plane(s) This is a word used in theosophy for the various ranges or steps of the hierarchical ladder of lives which blend into each other. There are no solutions of continuity in space, either in inner and invisible space or in outward and visible space. The physical world grades off into the astral world, which grades off again into a world higher than it, the world which is superior to the astral world; and so it continues throughout the series of hierarchical steps which compose a universe such as our universe. Remember also that the boundless All is filled full with universes, some so much greater than ours that the utmost reach of our imagination cannot conceive of them.

To quote H. P. Blavatsky in this connection, in her *Theosophical Glossary* under this same head:

"As used in Occultism, the term denotes the range or extent of some state of consciousness, or of the perceptive power of a particular set of senses, or the action of a particular force, or the state of matter corresponding to any of the above." (*See also* HIERARCHY)

Planetary Chain Every kosmic body or globe, be it sun or planet, nebula or comet, atom or electron, is a composite entity formed of or comprised of inner and invisible energies and substances and of an outer, to us, and often visible, to us, physical vehicle or body. These elements all together number seven (or twelve), being what is called in theosophy the seven principles or elements of every self-contained entity; in other words, of every individual life-center.

Thus every one of the physical globes that we see scattered over the fields of space is accompanied by six invisible and superior globes, forming what in theosophy is called a chain. This is the case with every sun or star, with every planet, and with every moon of every planet. It is likewise the case with the nebulae and the comets as above stated: all are septiform entities, all have a sevenfold constitution, even as man has, who is a copy in the little of what the universe is in the great, there being for us one life in that universe, one natural system of "laws" in that universe. Every entity in the universe is an inseparable part of it; therefore what is in the whole is in every part, because the part cannot contain anything that the whole does not contain, the part cannot be greater than the whole.

Our own earth-chain is composed of seven (or twelve) globes, of which only one, our earth, is visible on this our earth plane to our physical sense apparatus, because that apparatus is builded or rather evolved to cognize this earth plane and none other. But the populations of all the seven (or twelve) globes of this earth-chain pass in succession, and following each other, from globe to globe, thus gaining experience of energy and matter and consciousness on all the various planes and spheres that this chain comprises.

The other six (or eleven) globes of our earth-chain are invisible to our physical sense, of course; and, limiting our explanation only to the manifest seven globes of the complete chain of twelve globes, the six globes other and higher than the earth exist two by two, on three planes of the solar system superior to our physical plane where our earth-globe is — this our earth. These three superior planes or worlds are each one superior to the world or plane immediately beneath or inferior to it.

Our earth-globe is the fourth and lowest of all the manifest seven globes of our earth-chain. Three globes precede it on the descending or shadowy arc, and three globes follow it on the ascending or luminous arc of evolution. *The Secret Doctrine* by H. P. Blavatsky and the more recent work, *Fundamentals of the*

Esoteric Philosophy (1932), contain most suggestive material for the student interested in this phase of the esoteric philosophy. (*See also* ASCENDING ARC)

Planetary Spirit(s) Every celestial body in space, of whatever kind or type, is under the overseeing and directing influence of a hierarchy of spiritual and quasi-spiritual and astral beings, who in their aggregate are generalized under the name of celestial spirits. These celestial spirits exist therefore in various stages or degrees of evolution; but the term planetary spirits is usually restricted to the highest class of these beings when referring to a planet.

In every case, and whatever the celestial body may be, such a hierarchy of ethereal beings, when the most advanced in evolution of them are considered, in long past cycles of kosmic evolution had evolved through a stage of development corresponding to the humanity of earth. Every planetary spirit therefore, wherever existent, in those far past aeons of kosmic time was a man or a being equivalent to what we humans on earth call man. The planetary spirits of earth, for instance, are intimately linked with the origin and destiny of our present humanity, for not only are they our predecessors along the evolutionary path, but certain classes of them are actually the spiritual guides and instructors of mankind. We humans, in far distant aeons of the future, on a planetary chain which will be the child or grandchild of the present earth-chain, will be the planetary spirits of that future planetary chain. It is obvious that as H. P. Blavatsky says: "Our Earth, being as yet only in its Fourth Round, is far too young to have produced high Planetary Spirits"; but when the seventh round of this earth planetary chain shall have reached its end, our present humanity will then have become dhyān-chohans of various grades, planetary spirits of one group or class, with necessary evolutionary differences as among themselves. The planetary spirits watch over, guide, and lead the hosts of evolving entities inferior to themselves during the various rounds of a planetary chain. Finally, every celestial globe, whether sun or planet or other celestial body, has as the summit or acme of its spiritual hierarchy a supreme celestial spirit who is the hierarch of its own hierarchy. It should not be forgotten that the humanity of today forms a component element or stage or degree in the hierarchy of this (our) planetary chain.

Pradhāna *See* Prakṛiti

Prajāpati (Sanskrit) A word meaning "governor" or "lord" or "master" of "progeny." The word is applied to several of the Vedic gods, but in particular to Brahmā — that is to say the second step from parabrahman — the evolver-creator, the first and most recondite figure of the Hindu triad, consisting of Brahmā, Vishṇu, and Śiva. Brahmā is the emanator or evolver, Vishṇu the sustainer or preserver, and Śiva, a name which may be translated euphemistically perhaps as "beneficent," the regenerator. Prajāpati is a name which is often used in the plural, and refers to seven and also to ten different beings. They are the producers and givers of life of all on earth and, indeed, on the earth's planetary chain.

Prakṛiti (Sanskrit) A compound consisting of the prepositional prefix *pra,* meaning "forwards" or "progression," and *kṛiti,* a noun-form from the verbal root *kṛi,* "to make" or "to do." Therefore *prakṛiti* means literally "production" or "bringing forth," "originating," and by an extension of meaning it also signifies the primordial or original state or condition or form of anything: primary, original substance. The root or parent of prakṛiti is mūla-prakṛiti (q.v.) or root of prakṛiti. Prakṛiti is to be considered with *vikṛiti* — *vikṛiti* signifying change or an alteration of some kind, or a production or evolution from the *prakṛiti* which precedes it.

As an illustration, the chemical elements hydrogen and oxygen combine in the proportion H_2O, producing thus a substance known in its most common form as water; but this same H_2O can appear as ice as well as vapor-gas; hence the vapor, the water, and the ice may be called the vikṛitis of the original prakṛiti which is the originating hydrogen and oxygen. The illustration is perhaps not a very good one but is suggestive.

In common usage prakṛiti may be called nature in general, as the great producer of entities or things, and through this nature acts the ever-active Brahmā or Purusha. Purusha, therefore, is spirit, and prakṛiti is its productive veil or sheath. Essentially or fundamentally the two are one, and whatever prakṛiti through and by the influence of Purusha produces is the multitudinous and multiform vikṛitis which make the immense variety and diversity in the universe around us.

In one or more of the Hindu philosophies, prakṛiti is the same as śakti, and therefore prakṛiti and śakti are virtually interchangeable with māyā or mahā-māyā or so-called illusion. Prakṛiti is often spoken of as matter, but this is inexact although a very common usage; matter is rather the "productions" or phases that prakṛiti brings about, the vikṛitis. In the Indian Sānkhya philosophy pradhāna is virtually identical with prakṛiti, and both are often used to signify the producing element from and out of which all illusory material manifestations or appearances are evolved.

Pralaya (Sanskrit) A compound word, formed of *laya,* from the root *lī,* and the prefix *pra.* *Lī* means "to dissolve," "to melt away," "to liquefy," as when one pours water upon a cube of salt or of sugar. The cube of salt or of sugar vanishes in the water — it dissolves, changes its form — and this may be taken as a figure, imperfect as it is, or as a symbol, of what pralaya is: a crumbling away, a vanishing away, of matter into something else which is yet in it, and surrounds it, and interpenetrates it. Such is pralaya, usually translated as the state of latency, state of rest, state of repose, between two manvantaras (q.v.) or life cycles. If we remember distinctly the meaning of the Sanskrit word, our minds take a new bent in direction, follow a new thought. We get new ideas; we penetrate into the arcanum of the thing that takes place. Pralaya, therefore, is dissolution, death.

There are many kinds of pralayas. There is the universal pralaya, called *prākṛitika,* because it is the pralaya or vanishing away, melting away, of prakṛiti or nature. Then there is the solar pralaya. Sun in Sanskrit is *sūrya,* and the adjective from this is *saurya*: hence, the saurya pralaya or the pralaya of the solar system. Then, thirdly, there is the terrestrial or planetary pralaya. One Sanskrit word for earth is *bhūmi,* and the adjective corresponding to this is *bhaumika*: hence, the bhaumika pralaya. Then there is the pralaya or death of the individual man. Man is *purusha*; the corresponding adjective is *paurusha*: hence, the paurusha pralaya or death of man. These adjectives apply equally well to the several kinds of manvantaras or life cycles.

There is another kind of pralaya which is called *nitya.* In its general sense, it means "constant" or "continuous," and can be exemplified by the constant or continuous change — life and death — of the cells of our bodies. It is a state in which the indwelling and dominating entity remains, but its different principles and *rūpas* undergo continuous and incessant change. Hence it is called *nitya,* signifying continuous. It applies to the body of man, to the outer sphere of earth, to the earth itself, to the solar system, and indeed to all nature. It is the unceasing and chronic changing of things that are — the passing from phase to phase, meaning the pralaya or death of one phase, to be followed by the rebirth of its succeeding phase. There are other kinds of pralayas than those herein enumerated.

Prāṇa (Sanskrit) The word is derived from *pra,* prepositional prefix meaning "before"; and *an,* verb meaning "to breathe," "to blow," "to live." Usually translated "life," but rather the psychoelectrical veil or psychoelectrical field manifesting in the individual as vitality. Commonly called "life principle." This Sanskrit word is used by modern theosophists in a *general* sense, although in the Sanskrit it has a rather specific and restricted meaning, because there are, as a matter of fact, a number of life currents, vital fluids. They have each one its own name. One system gives the number as three; another as five, which is the commonly accepted number; another enumeration is seven; another again is twelve, as is found in some Upanishads; and one old writer even gives them as thirteen.

The life-atoms of the prāṇa, or psychoelectrical field, fly instantly back at the moment of physical dissolution to the natural prāṇic reservoirs of the planet.

Prāṇāyāma *See* SAMĀDHI

Pratyāhāra *See* SAMĀDHI

Pratyeka Buddha (Sanskrit) *Pratyeka* is a compound of two words: *prati,* prepositional prefix meaning "towards" or "for"; *eka,* the numeral "one"; thus we can translate the compound by the paraphrase "each one for himself."

The Pratyeka Buddha, he who achieves buddhahood for himself, instead of feeling the call of almighty love to return and help those who have gone less far, goes ahead into the supernal light — passes onwards and enters the unspeakable bliss of nirvāṇa — and leaves mankind behind. Though exalted, nevertheless he does not rank with the unutterable sublimity of the Buddha of Compassion (q.v.).

The Pratyeka Buddha concentrates his energies on the one objective — spiritual self-advancement: he raises himself to the spiritual realm of his own inner being, enwraps himself therein and, so to speak, goes to sleep. The Buddha of Compassion raises himself, as does the Pratyeka Buddha, to the spiritual realms of his own inner being, but does not stop there, because he expands continuously, becomes one with All, or tries to, and in fact does so in time. When the Pratyeka Buddha in due course emerges from the nirvāṇic state in order to take up his evolutionary journey again, he will find himself far in the rear of the Buddha of Compassion.

Pravṛitti *See* EVOLUTION; *also* INVOLUTION

Preexistence This term means that the human soul did not first come into being or existence with its present birth on earth; in other words, that it preexisted before it was born on earth.

This doctrine of preexistence is by no means typically theosophical, for it likewise was a part of the early teachings of Christianity, as is evidenced in the writings that remain to us of Origen, the great Alexandrian Church Father, and of his school. The theosophical student should be very careful in distinguishing the technical meanings that pertain to several words which in popular and mistaken usage are often employed interchangeably, as for example preexistence, metempsychosis, transmigration, reincarnation, reimbodiment, rebirth, metensomatosis, palingenesis. Each one of these words has a specific meaning typically its own, and describes or sets forth one phase of the destiny of a reimbodying and migrating entity. In popular usage, several of these words are used as synonyms, and this usage is wrong. Preexistence, for instance, does not necessarily signify the transmigration of an entity from plane to plane nor, indeed, does it signify as does reincarnation that a migrating monad reinfleshes or reincarnates itself through its ray on earth. Preexistence signifies only that a soul, be it human or other, preexisted before its birth on earth.

The doctrine of the great Origen, as found in his works that remain to us, was that the human soul preexisted in the spiritual world, or within the influence or range of the divine essence or "God," before it began a series of reincarnations on earth. It is obvious that Origen's manner of expressing his views is a more or less faithful but distorted reflection of the teaching of the esoteric philosophy. The teaching of preexistence as outlined by Origen and his school and followers, with others of his mystical quasi-theosophical doctrines, was formally condemned and anathematized at the Home Synod held under Mennas at Constantinople about 543 of the Christian era. Thus passed out of orthodox Christian theology as a "newly discovered heresy" what was a most important and mystical body of teaching of the early centuries of the new Christian religion — to the latter's great loss, spiritual and intellectual. The doctrines of Origen and his school may be said to have formed an important part of original Christian theosophy, a form of universal theosophy of Christianized character. (See under their respective heads the various correlated doctrines mentioned above.)

Principles of Man The seven principles of man are a likeness or rather copy of the seven cosmic principles. They are actually the offspring or reflection of the seven cosmic principles, limited in their action in us by the workings of the law of karma, but running in their origin back into THAT which is beyond: into THAT which is the essence of the universe or the universal — above, beyond, within, to the unmanifest, to the unmanifestable, to that first principle which H. P. Blavatsky enunciates as the leading thought of the wisdom-philosophy of *The Secret Doctrine.*

These principles of man are reckoned as seven in the philosophy by which the human spiritual and psychical economy has been publicly explained to us in the present age. In other ages these principles or parts of man were differently reckoned — the Christian reckoned them as body, soul, and spirit, generalizing the seven under these three heads.

Some of the Indian thinkers divided man into a basic fourfold entity, others into a fivefold. The Jewish philosophy, as found in the Qabbālāh which is the esoteric tradition of the Jews, teaches that man is divided into four parts: *neshāmāh, rūaḥ, nefesh,* and *gūf.*

Theosophists for convenience often employ in their current literature a manner of viewing man's composite constitution which is the dividing of his nature into a trichotomy, meaning a division into three, being spirit, soul, and body, which in this respect is identical with the generalized Christianized theosophical division. Following this trichotomy, man's three parts, therefore, are: first and highest, the divine spirit or the divine monad of him, which is rooted in the universe, which spirit is linked with the All, being in a highly mystical sense a ray of the All; second, the intermediate part, or the spiritual monad, which in its higher and lower aspects is the spiritual and human souls; then, third, the lowest part of man's composite constitution, the vital-astral-physical part of him, which is composed of material or quasi-material life-atoms. (*See also* Ātman, Buddhi, Manas, Kāma, Prāṇa, Liṅga-Śarīra, Sthūla-Śarīra)

Psychic Powers The lowest powers of the intermediate or soul-nature in the human being, and we are exercising and using them all the time — yes, and we cannot even control them properly! Men's emotional thoughts are vagrant, wandering, uncertain, lacking precision, without positive direction, and feebly governed. The average man cannot even keep his emotions and thoughts in the grip of his self-conscious will. His weakest passions lead him astray. It is this part of his nature whence flow his "psychic powers." It is man's work to transmute them and to turn them to employment which is good and useful and holy. Indeed, the average man cannot control the ordinary psycho-astral-physical powers that he commonly uses; and when, forsooth, people talk about cultivating occult powers, by which they mean merely psychic powers, it simply shows that through ignorance they know not to what they refer. Their minds are clouded as regards the actual facts. Those who talk so glibly of cultivating occult powers are just the people who cannot be trusted as real guides, for before they themselves can crawl in these mysterious regions of life, they seem to desire to teach other people how to run and to leap. What most people really mean, apparently, when they speak of cultivating occult powers is "I want to get power over other people." Such individuals are totally unfit to wield occult powers of any kind, for the motive is in most cases purely selfish, and their minds are beclouded and darkened with ignorance.

The so-called psychic powers have the same relation to genuine *spiritual powers* that baby-talk has to the discourse of a wise philosopher. Before occult powers of any kind can be cultivated safely, man must learn the first lesson of the mystic knowledge, which is to control himself; and all powers that later he gains must be laid on the altar of impersonal service — on the altar of service to mankind.

Psychic powers will come to men as a natural development of their inner faculties, as evolution performs its wonderful work in future ages. New senses, and new organs corresponding to these new senses, both interior and exterior, will come into active functioning in the distant future. But it is perilous both to sanity and to health to attempt to force the development of these prematurely, and unless the training and discipline be done under the watchful and compassionate eye of a genuine occult teacher who knows what he is about. The world even today contains hundreds of thousands of "sensitives" who are the first feeble forerunners of what future evolution will make common in the human race; but these sensitives are usually in a very unfortunate and trying situation, for they themselves misunderstand what is in them, and they are misunderstood by their fellows. (*See also* OCCULTISM)

Psychology This word is ordinarily used to signify in our days, and in the seats of learning in the Occident, a study mostly beclouded with doubts and hypotheses, and often actual guesswork, meaning little more than a kind of mental physiology, practically nothing more than the working of the brain-mind in the lowest astral-psychical apparatus of the human constitution. But in the theosophical philosophy, the word psychology is used to mean something very different and of a far nobler character: we might call it pneumatology, or the science or the study of spirit and its rays, because all the inner faculties and powers of man ultimately spring from his spiritual nature. The term psychology ought really to connote the study of the inner intermediate economy of man, and the interconnection of his principles and elements or centers of energy or force — what the man really is inwardly.

In days of the far bygone past, psychology was indeed what the word signifies: "the science of soul"; and upon this science was securely based the collateral and subordinate science of genuine physiology. Today, however, it is physiology which serves as the basis for psychology because of a mistaken view of man's constitution. It is a case of *hysteron proteron* — putting the cart before the horse.

Purāṇas (Sanskrit) A word which literally means "ancient," "belonging to olden times." In India the word is especially used as a term comprehending certain well-known sacred scriptures, which popular and even scholarly authorities ascribe to the poet Vyāsa. The Purāṇas contain the entire body of ancient Indian mythology. They are usually considered to be eighteen in number, and each Purāṇa, to be complete, is supposed to consist of five topics or themes. These five topics or themes are commonly enumerated as follows: (1) the beginnings or "creation" of the universe; (2) its renewals and destructions, or manvantaras and pralayas; (3) the genealogies of the gods, other divine beings, heroes, and patriarchs; (4) the reigns of the various manus; and (5) a résumé of the history of the solar and lunar races. Practically none of the Purāṇas as they stand in modern versions contains all these five topics, except perhaps the *Vishṇu-Purāṇa,* probably the most complete in this sense of the word; and even the *Vishṇu-Purāṇa* contains a great deal of matter not directly to be classed under these five topics. All the Purāṇas also contain a great deal of symbolical and allegorical writing.

Purusha (Sanskrit) A word meaning "man," the Ideal Man, like the Qabbalistic Ādām Qadmōn, the primordial entity of space, containing with and in prakṛiti (q.v.) or nature all the septenary (or denary) scales of manifested being. More mystically Purusha has a number of different significancies. In addition to meaning the Heavenly Man or Ideal Man, it is frequently used for the spiritual man in each individual human being or, indeed, in every self-conscious entity — therefore a term for the spiritual self.

Purusha also sometimes stands as an interchangeable term with Brahmā, the evolver or "creator."

Probably the simplest and most inclusive significance of Purusha as properly used in the esoteric philosophy is expressed in the paraphrase "the entitative, individual, everlasting divine-spiritual self," the spiritual monad, whether of a universe or of a solar system, or of an individual entity in manifested life, such as man.

— Q —

Qabbālāh (More frequently spelled *Kabala* or *Kabbala.*) The Hebrew word for what the Jewish theosophical initiates called "the Tradition," or "the Secret Doctrine" — meaning something which is handed down or passed down from man to man by tradition; from a Hebrew word meaning "to receive" or "to take over."

Unquestionably the Jewish Qabbālāh existed as a traditional system of doctrine long before the present manuscripts of it were written, for these are of comparatively late production and probably date from the European Middle Ages; and one proof of this statement is found in the fact that in the earliest centuries of the Christian era several of the Church Fathers of the new Christian religion used language which could have been taken only from the Hebrew theosophy, that is, the Hebrew Qabbālāh. The expressions here are in some cases identic, and the thought is in all cases the same.

The *Zohar* may be called the original and main book of the Qabbālāh.

The basis of the Jewish Qabbālāh was the archaic Chaldean secret doctrine which was a system of occult or esoteric philosophy handed down in part by oral, and in part by written, transmission — and mostly by oral reception, wholly so in the case of the deeper mysteries of the Qabbālāh. The Jewish Qabbālāh, such as it exists today, has been disfigured and distorted by the interpolations and mutilations of many Western occultists, especially by mystics of strong Christian bias. The Qabbālāh, therefore, is essentially the theosophy of the Jews, or rather the form which the universal theosophy of the archaic ages took in its transmission through the Jewish mind.

— R —

Races During evolution on our earth (and on the other six manifest globes of the planetary chain of earth correspondentially), mankind as a life-wave passes through seven evolutionary stages called root-races. Seven such root-races form the evolutionary cycle on this globe earth in this fourth round through the planetary chain; and this evolutionary cycle through our globe earth is called one globe round. We are at the present time in the fourth subrace of our present fifth root-race, on globe D or our earth.

Each root-race is divided in our teachings into seven minor races, and each one of these seven minor races is again in its turn subdivided into seven branchlet or still smaller racial units, etc.

The student who is interested in the matter of tracing the evolutionary arrangement or history of the seven root-races on our globe earth is referred primarily to H. P. Blavatsky's *The Secret Doctrine*, and secondarily to *Fundamentals of the Esoteric Philosophy.*

Each one of the seven root-races reaches its maximum of material efflorescence and power at about its middle point. When half of the cycle of any one of the seven root-races is run, then the racial cataclysm ensues, for such is the way in which nature operates; and at this middle racial point, at the middle point of the fourth subrace of the mother-race or root-race, a new root-race begins or is born out of the preceding root-race, and pursues its evolution from birth towards maturity, side by side with, or rather in connection with, the latter half of the preceding mother-race or root-race. It is in this fashion that the root-races overlap each other, a most interesting fact in ethnological or racial history. This overlapping likewise takes place in the cases of the minor and branchlet races.

It will be between sixteen thousand and twenty thousand years more before the racial cataclysm will ensue which will cut our own fifth root-race in two — exactly as the same racial cataclysmic occurrence happened to the fourth-race Atlanteans who preceded us, and to the third-race Lemurians who preceded them; and as it will happen to the two root-races which will follow ours, the sixth and seventh — for we are now approaching the middle point of our own fifth root-race, because we are nearing the middle point of the fourth subrace of this fifth root-race. (*See also* GLOBE, PLANETARY CHAIN, ROUND)

Rajas (Sanskrit) One of the three guṇas or "qualities" in the correlations of force and matter, the other two being respectively sattva (q.v.) and tamas (q.v.). Rajas is the guṇa or the "quality" of longing, passion, activity, one of the three divisions of nature. In a sense it is the result or consequence of the elementary urge in nature producing change and the longing therefor.

Rāja Yoga *See* YOGA

Rebirth One of the several aspects or branches of the general doctrine of reimbodiment. A word of large and generalized significance. Signifying merely a succession of rebirths, the definition becomes generalized, excluding specific explanations as to the type or kind of reimbodiment. The likeness between the idea comprised in this word and that belonging to the term reincarnation is very close, yet the two ideas are quite distinct. (For this difference *see* REINCARNATION; *also* PREEXISTENCE, METEMPSYCHOSIS, TRANSMIGRATION, etc.)

Rechaka (*Recaka*, Sanskrit) One of the practices used in the haṭha yoga system for the regulation of the breath. The breath is expelled or expired from one of the nostrils while the other nostril is held closed with the finger, and then the operation is repeated with the other nostril. These operations, as observed under Kumbhaka (q.v.), are extremely dangerous to health and mental balance, and cannot be encouraged. Indeed, they should be unequivocally discouraged.

Reimbodiment This term means that the living and migrating entity takes upon itself a new body at some time after death. Its meaning, therefore, is a highly generalized one, and the specific significance is that of assuming new imbodiments periodically. It teaches something more than that the soul merely preexists, the idea being that the soul takes unto itself a succession of new bodies — on whatever plane it may happen to be. This particular aspect or branch of the general doctrine of the migration of living entities tells us not what kind of body the soul newly assumes, nor whether that body be taken here on earth or elsewhere, that is to say, whether the new body is to be a visible body or an invisible one in the invisible realms of nature. It simply says that the life-center *reimbodies* itself; and this is the essence of the specific meaning of this word. (*See also* Preexistence, Rebirth, Metempsychosis, Reincarnation, etc.)

Reincarnating Ego In the method of dividing the human principles into a trichotomy of an upper duad, an intermediate duad, and a lower triad — or distributively spirit, soul, and body — the second or intermediate duad, manas-kāma, or the intermediate nature, is the ordinary seat of human consciousness, and itself is composed of two qualitative parts: an upper or aspiring part, which is commonly called the reincarnating ego or the higher manas, and a lower part attracted to material things, which is the focus of what expresses itself in the average man as the human ego, his everyday ordinary seat of consciousness.

When death occurs, the mortal and material portions sink into oblivion; while the reincarnating ego carries the best and noblest parts of the spiritual memory of the man that was into the devachan (q.v.) or heaven world of postmortem rest and recuperation, where the ego remains in the bosom of the monad or of the monadic essence in a state of the most perfect and utter bliss and peace, constantly reviewing and improving upon in its own blissful imagination all the unfulfilled spiritual yearnings and longings of the life just closed that its naturally creative faculties automatically suggest to the entity now in the devachan.

But the monad above spoken of passes from sphere to sphere on its peregrinations from earth, carrying with it the reincarnating ego, or what we may for simplicity of expression call the earth-child, in its bosom, where this reincarnating ego is in its state of perfect bliss and peace, until the time comes when, having passed through all the invisible realms connected by chains of causation with our own planet, it slowly "descends" again through these higher intermediate spheres earthwards. Coincidently does the reincarnating ego slowly begin to reawaken to self-conscious activity. Gradually it feels, at first unconsciously to itself, the attraction earthwards, arising out of the karmic seeds of thought and emotion and impulse sown in the preceding life on earth and now beginning to awaken; and as these attractions grow stronger, in other words as the reincarnating ego awakens more fully, it finds itself under the domination of a strong psychomagnetic attraction drawing it to the earth-sphere.

The time finally comes when it is drawn strongly to the family on earth whose karmic attractions or karmic status or condition are the nearest to its own characteristics; and it then enters, or attaches itself to, by reason of the psychomagnetic attraction, the human seed which will grow into the body of the human being to be. Thus reincarnation takes place, and the reincarnating ego reawakens to life on earth in the body of a little child.

Reincarnation An anglicized word of Latin derivation, meaning "reinfleshment," the coming again into a human body of an excarnate human soul. The repetitive reimbodiment of the reincarnating human ego in vehicles of human flesh — this being a special case of the general doctrine of reimbodiment. This general doctrine of reimbodiment applies not solely to man, but to all centers of consciousness whatsoever, or to all monads whatsoever — wheresoever they may be on the evolutionary ladder of life, and whatsoever may be their particular developmental grade thereon.

The meaning of this general doctrine is very simple indeed. It is as follows: every life-consciousness-center, in other words, every monad or monadic essence, reincorporates itself repeatedly in various vehicles or bodies, to use the popular word. These bodies may be spiritual, or they may be physical, or they may be of a nature intermediate between these two, i.e., ethereal. This rule of nature, which applies to all monads without exception, takes place in all the different realms of the visible and invisible universe, and on all its different planes, and in all its different worlds.

There are eight words used in the theosophical philosophy in connection with reimbodiment, which are not all synonymous, although some of these eight words have almost the same specific meaning. They are: preexistence, rebirth, reimbodiment, palingenesis, metensomatosis, metempsychosis, transmigration, reincarnation (see under each word for definition). Of these eight words, four only may be said to contain the four different basic ideas of the general doctrine of reimbodiment, and these four are preexistence, reimbodiment, metempsychosis, and transmigration.

In no case is the word reincarnation *identical* with any of the other seven words, though of course it has grounds of strong similarity with them all, as for instance with preexistence, because obviously the entity preexists before it reincarnates; and on the same grounds it is similar to rebirth, reimbodiment, and metensomatosis.

The meaning of the word reincarnation differs specifically from rebirth in this, that the latter word simply means rebirth in human bodies of flesh on this earth; while the former term also contains the implication, tacit if not expressed, of possible incarnations in flesh by entities which have finished their earthly pilgrimage or evolution, but who can and sometimes do return to this earth in order to incarnate for the purpose of aiding their less evolved brothers.

Relativity The modern scientific doctrine of relativity, despite its restrictions and mathematical limitations, is extremely suggestive because it introduces metaphysics into physics, does away with purely speculative ideas that certain things are absolute in a purely relative universe, and brings us back to an examination of nature as nature is and not as mathematical theorists have hitherto tacitly taken it to be. The doctrine of relativity in its essential idea of relations rather than absolutes is true; but this does not mean that we necessarily accept Einstein's or his followers' deductions. These latter may or may not be true, and time will show. In any case, relativity is not what it is often misunderstood to be — the naked doctrine that "everything is relative," which would mean that there is nothing fundamental or basic or real anywhere, whence other things flow forth; in other words, that there is no positively real or fundamental divine and spiritual background of being. The relativity theory is an adumbration, a reaching out for, a groping after, a very, very old theosophical doctrine — the doctrine of māyā (q.v.).

The manner in which theosophy teaches the conception of relativity is that while the universe is a relative universe and all its parts are therefore relative — each to each, and each to all, and all to each — yet there is a deathless reality behind, which forms the substratum or the truth of things, out of which the phenomenal in all its myriad relative manifestations flows. And there is a way, a road, a path, by which men may reach this reality behind, because it is in man as his inmost essence and therefore primal origin. In each one is fundamentally this reality of which we are all in search. Each one is the path that leads to it, for it is the heart of the universe.

In a sense still more metaphysical, even the heart of a universe may be said to exist relatively in connection with other universes with their hearts. It would be quite erroneous to suppose that there is one Absolute Reality in the old-fashioned European sense, and that all relative manifestations flow forth from it, and that these relative manifestations although derived from this Absolute Reality are without links of union or origin with an Absolute (q.v.) even still more essential and fundamental and vaster. Once the conception of boundless infinitude is grasped, the percipient intelligence immediately realizes that it is simply hopeless, indeed impossible, to postulate ends, absolute Absolutes, as the divine *ultima thule.* No matter how vast and kosmic an Absolute may be, there are in sheer frontierless infinitude always innumerable other Absolutes equal to or greater than it.

Religion An operation of the human spiritual mind in its endeavor to understand not only the *how* and the *why* of things, but comprising in addition a yearning and striving towards self-conscious union with the divine All and an endlessly growing self-conscious identification with the cosmic divine-spiritual realities. One phase of a triform method of understanding the nature of nature, of universal nature, and its multiform and multifold workings; and this phase cannot be separated from the other two phases (science and philosophy) if we wish to gain a true picture of things *as they are in themselves.*

Human religion is the expression of that aspect of man's consciousness which is intuitional, aspirational, and mystical, and which is often deformed and distorted in its lower forms by the emotional in man.

It is usual among modern Europeans to derive the word religion from the Latin verb meaning "to bind back" — *religare.* But there is another derivation, which is the one that Cicero chooses, and of course he was a Roman himself and had great skill and deep knowledge in the use of his own native tongue. This other derivation comes from a Latin root meaning "to select," "to choose," from which, likewise, we have the word *lex,* "law," i.e., the course of conduct or rule of action which is chosen as the best, and is therefore followed; in other words, that which is the best of its kind, as ascertained by selection, by trial, and by proof.

Thus then, the meaning of the word religion from the Latin *religio,* means a careful selection of fundamental beliefs and motives by the higher or spiritual intellect, a faculty of intuitional judgment and understanding, and a consequent abiding by that selection, resulting in a course of life and conduct in all respects following the convictions that have been arrived at. This is the religious spirit.

To this the theosophist would add the following very important idea: behind all the various religions and philosophies of ancient times there is a secret or esoteric wisdom given out by the greatest men who have ever lived, the founders and builders of the various world religions and world philosophies; and this sublime system in fundamentals has been the same everywhere over the face of the globe.

This system has passed under various names, e.g., the esoteric philosophy, the ancient wisdom, the secret doctrine, the traditional teaching, theosophy, etc. (*See also* SCIENCE, PHILOSOPHY)

Right-hand Path From time immemorial, in all countries of the earth, among all races of men, there have been existent two opposing and antagonistic schools of occult or esoteric training, the one often technically called the Path of Light, and the other the Path of Darkness or of the Shadows. These two paths likewise are much more commonly called the right-hand path and the left-hand path, and although these are technical names in the rather shaky occultism of the Occident, the very same expressions have prevailed all over the world, and are especially known in the mystical and esoteric literature of Hindustan. The right-hand path is known in Sanskrit writings by the name *dakshiṇa-mārga*, and those who practice the rules of conduct and follow the manner of life enjoined upon those who follow the right-hand path are technically known as *dakshiṇāchārins,* and their course of life is known as *dakshiṇāchāra.* Conversely, those who follow the left-hand path, often called Brothers of the Shadow, or by some similar epithet, are called *vāmāchārins,* and their school or course of life is known as *vāmāchāra.* An alternative expression for *vāmāchāra* is *savyāchāra.* The white magicians or Brothers of Light are therefore *dakshiṇāchārins,* and the black magicians or Brothers of the Shadow, or workers of spiritual and intellectual and psychical evil, are therefore *vāmāchārins*.

To speak in the mystical language of ancient Greece, the *dakshiṇāchārins* or Brothers of Light pursue the winding ascent to Olympus, whereas the *vāmāchārins* or Brothers of the Left-hand follow the easy but fearfully perilous path leading downwards into ever more confusing, horrifying stages of matter and spiritual obscuration. The latter is the *faciles descensus averno* (*Aeneid*, 6.126) of the Latin poet Virgil. Woe be to him who, refusing to raise his soul to the sublime and cleansing rays of the spiritual sun within him, places his feet upon the path which leads downwards. The warnings given to students of occultism about this matter have always been solemn and urgent, and no esotericist should at any moment consider himself safe or beyond the possibilities of taking the downward way until he has become at one with the divine monitor within his own breast, his own inner god.

Ring-Pass-Not A profoundly mystical and suggestive term signifying the circle or bounds or frontiers within which is contained the consciousness of those who are still under the sway of the delusion of separateness — and this applies whether the ring be large or small. It does not signify any one especial occasion or condition, but is a general term applicable to any state in which an entity, having reached a certain stage of evolutionary growth of the unfolding of consciousness, finds itself unable to pass into a still higher state because of some delusion under which the consciousness is laboring, be that delusion mental or spiritual. There is consciously a ring-pass-not for every globe of the planetary chain, a ring-pass-not for the planetary chain itself, a ring-pass-not for the solar system, and so forth. It is the entities who labor under the delusion who therefore actually create their own rings-pass-not, for these are not actual entitative material frontiers, but boundaries of consciousness.

A ring-pass-not furthermore may perhaps be said with great truth to be somewhat of the nature of a spiritual laya-center (q.v.)

or point of transmission between plane and plane of consciousness.

The rings-pass-not as above said, however, have to do with phases or states of consciousness only. For instance, the ring-pass-not for the beasts is self-consciousness, i.e., the beasts have not yet been enabled to develop forth their consciousness to the point of self-consciousness or reflective consciousness except in minor degree. A dog, for example, located in a room which it desires to leave, will run to a door out of which it is accustomed to go and will sit there whining for the door to be opened. Its consciousness recognizes the point of egress, but it has not developed the self-conscious mental activity to open the door.

A general ring-pass-not for humanity is their inability to self-consciously participate in spiritual self-consciousness.

Root-Race *See* RACES

Round The doctrine concerning our planetary chain commonly called that of the seven rounds means that the life cycle or life-wave begins its evolutionary course on globe A, the first of the series of seven (or ten) globes; then, completing its cycles there, runs down to globe B, and then to globe C, and then to globe D, our earth; and then, on the ascending arc (q.v.), to globe E, then to globe F, and then to globe G. These are the manifest seven globes of the planetary chain. This is one *planetary round.* After the planetary round there ensues a planetary or chain nirvāṇa, until the second round begins in the same way, but in a more "advanced" degree of evolution than was the first round.

A *globe round* is one of the seven passages of a life-wave during its planetary round, on any one (and therefore on and through each) of the globes. When the life-wave has passed through globe D, for instance, and ends its cycles on globe D, this is the globe round of globe D for that particular planetary round; and so with all the globes respectively. Seven root-races make one globe round. There are seven globe rounds therefore (one globe round for each of the seven globes) in each planetary round.

Seven planetary rounds equal one kalpa or manvantara or Day of Brahmā. When seven planetary rounds have been accomplished, which is as much as saying forty-nine globe rounds (or globe manvantaras), there ensues a still higher nirvāṇa than that occurring between globes G and A after each planetary round. This higher nirvāṇa is coincident with what is called a pralaya of that planetary chain, which pralaya lasts until the cycle again returns for a new planetary chain to form, containing the same hosts of living beings as on the preceding chain, and which are now destined to enter upon the new planetary chain, but on and in a higher series of planes or worlds than in the preceding one.

When seven such planetary chains with their various kalpas or manvantaras have passed away, this sevenfold grand cycle is one solar manvantara, and then the solar system sinks into the solar or cosmic pralaya.

There are outer rounds and inner rounds. An inner round comprises the passage of the life-wave in any one planetary chain from globe A to globe G once around, and this takes place seven times in a planetary manvantara.

The outer round comprises the passage of the entirety of a life-wave of a planetary chain along the circulations of the solar system, from one of the seven sacred planets to another; and this for seven (or ten) times.

There is another aspect of the teaching concerning the outer rounds which cannot be elucidated here.

Rūpa (Sanskrit) A word meaning "form," "image," "similitude," but this word is employed technically, and only rarely in the popular sense in which it is commonly used in English. It signifies rather an atomic or monadic aggregation about the central and indwelling consciousness, forming a vehicle or body thereof.

Thus the rūpa-lokas are lokas or worlds where the body-form or vehicle is very definitely outlined in matter; whereas the arūpa-lokas are worlds where the body-forms or "images" are outlined in a manner which *to us humans* is much less definite. It should be noted that the word rūpa applies with equal force to the bodies or vehicles even of the gods, although these latter to us are purely subjective or arūpa (q.v.). (*See also* LOKA)

— S —

Śabda-Brahman (Sanskrit) A phrase literally signifying "Word-Brahman" — a curious analogy with the archaic Greek mystical teaching concerning the Logos. Śabda-Brahman, therefore, may be rendered as the active unmanifest Logos of the solar system, and hence as the soul of Brahman expressing itself through its ākāśic veils as the divine Logos, or Word or Sound. This term is closely connected in meaning with the teaching concerning daivīprakṛiti (q.v.). H. P. Blavatsky in her posthumous *Glossary* speaks of the Śabda-Brahman as "Ethereal Vibrations diffused throughout Space."

Śakti (Sanskrit) A term which may be briefly defined to mean one of what in modern Occultism are called the seven forces of nature, of which six are manifest and the seventh unmanifest, or only partly manifest. Śakti in general may be described as universal energy, and is, as it were, the feminine aspect of fohat (q.v.). In popular Hinduism the various śaktis are the wives or consorts of the gods, in other words, the energies or active powers of the deities represented as feminine influences or energies.

These anthropomorphic definitions are unfortunate, because misleading. The śaktis of nature are really the veils, or sheaths, or vehicular carriers, through which work the inner and ever-active energies. As substance and energy, or force and matter, are fundamentally one, as modern science in its researches has begun to discover, it becomes apparent that even these śaktis or sheaths or veils are themselves energic to lower spheres or realms through which they themselves work.

The crown of the astral light (q.v.), as H. P. Blavatsky puts it, is the generalized śakti of universal nature in so far as our solar system is concerned.

Samādhi (Sanskrit) A compound word formed of *sam*, meaning "with" or "together"; *ā*, meaning "towards"; and the verbal root *dhā*, signifying "to place," or "to bring"; hence *samādhi*, meaning "to direct towards," generally signifies to combine the faculties of the mind with a direction towards an object. Hence, intense contemplation or profound meditation, with the consciousness directed to the spiritual. It is the highest form of self-possession, in the sense of collecting all the faculties of the constitution towards reaching union or quasi-union, long or short in time as the case may be, with the divine-spiritual. One who possesses and is accustomed to use this power has complete, absolute control over all his faculties, and is, therefore, said to be "completely *self*-possessed." It is the highest state of yoga (q.v.) or "union."

Samādhi, therefore, is a word of exceedingly mystical and profound significance implying the complete abstraction of the percipient consciousness from all worldly or exterior or even mental concerns or attributes, and its absorption into or, perhaps better, its becoming the pure unadulterate, undilute superconsciousness of the god within. In other words, samādhi is self-conscious union with the spiritual monad of the human constitution. Samādhi is the eighth or final stage of genuine occult yoga, and can be attained at any time by the initiate without conscious recourse to the other phases or practices of yoga enumerated in Oriental works, and which other and inferior practices are often misleading, in some cases distinctly injurious, and at the best mere props or aids in the attaining of complete mental abstraction from worldly concerns.

The eight stages of yoga usually enumerated are the following: (1) *yama*, signifying "restraint" or "forbearance"; (2) *niyama*, religious observances of various kinds, such as watchings or fastings, prayings, penances, etc.; (3) *āsana* (q.v.), postures of various kinds; (4) *prāṇāyāma*, various methods of regulating the breath;

(5) *pratyāhāra*, a word signifying "withdrawal," but technically and esoterically the "withdrawal" of the consciousness from sensual or sensuous concerns, or from external objects; (6) *dhāraṇā* (q.v.), firmness or steadiness or resolution in holding the mind set or concentrated on a topic or object of thought, mental concentration; (7) *dhyāna* (q.v.), abstract contemplation or meditation when freed from exterior distractions; and finally, (8) *samādhi*, complete collection of the consciousness and of its faculties into oneness or union with the monadic essence.

It may be observed, and should be carefully taken note of by the student, that when the initiate has attained samādhi he becomes practically omniscient for the solar universe in which he dwells, because his consciousness is functioning at the time in the spiritual-causal worlds. All knowledge is then to him like an open page because he is self-consciously conscious, to use a rather awkward phrase, of nature's inner and spiritual realms, the reason being that his consciousness has become kosmic in its reaches.

Śambhala (Sanskrit) A place-name of highly mystical significance. Many learned occidental Orientalists have endeavored to identify this mystical and unknown locality with some well-known modern district or town, but unsuccessfully. The name is mentioned in the Purāṇas and elsewhere, and it is stated that out of Śambhala will appear in due course of time the Kalki-Avatāra of the future. The Kalki-Avatāra is one of the manifestations or avatāras of Vishṇu. Among the Buddhists it is also stated that out of Śambhala will come in due course of time the Maitreya-Buddha or next buddha.

Śambhala, however, although no erudite Orientalist has yet succeeded in locating it geographically, is an actual land or district, the seat of the greatest brotherhood of spiritual adepts and their chiefs on earth today. From Śambhala at certain times in the history of the world, or more accurately of our own fifth root-race, come forth the messengers or envoys for spiritual and intellectual work among men.

This Great Brotherhood has branches in various parts of the world, but Śambhala is the center or chief lodge. We may tentatively locate it in a little-known and remote district of the high tablelands of central Asia, more particularly in Tibet. A multitude of airplanes might fly over the place without "seeing" it, for its frontiers are very carefully guarded and protected against invasion, and will continue to be so until the karmic destiny of our present fifth root-race brings about a change of location to some other spot on the earth, which then in its turn will be as carefully guarded as Śambhala now is.

Sambhogakāya (Sanskrit) This is a compound of two words meaning "enjoyment-body," or rather "participation-body"; *sambhoga* meaning "enjoyment together," or "delightful participation," etc.; and *kāya*, meaning "body." This is the second of the glorious vestures, the other two being *dharmakāya* (q.v.), the highest, and *nirmāṇakāya* (q.v.), the lowest. The buddha in the sambhogakāya state still participates in, still retains more or less, his self-consciousness as an individual, his egoship and his individual soul-sense, though he is too far above material or personal concerns to care about or to meddle with them. In consequence, a buddha in the sambhogakāya state would be virtually powerless here on our material earth.

Sannyāsin (Sanskrit) One who renounces (a renouncer); from *sannyāsa*, "renunciation," abandonment of worldly bonds and attractions. Resignation to the service of the spiritual nature.

Śarīra (Sanskrit) From a root which can best be translated by saying that it means what is easily dissolved, easily worn away; the idea being something transitory, foam-like, full of holes, as it were. Note the meaning hid in this — it is very important. A term which is of common usage in the philosophy of Hindustan, and of very frequent usage in modern theosophical philosophy. A general meaning is a composite body or vehicle of impermanent character in and through which an ethereal entity lives and works. (*See also* LIṄGA-ŚARĪRA, STHŪLA-ŚARĪRA)

Sat (Sanskrit) A word meaning the real, the enduring fundamental essence of the world. In the ancient Brahmanical teachings the terms *sat, chit, ānanda,* were used to signify the state of what one may call the Absolute: *sat* meaning "pure being"; *chit,* "pure thought"; *ānanda,* "bliss," and these three words were compounded as *sachchidānanda.* (*See also* ASAT)

Sattva (Sanskrit) One of the *triguṇas* or "three qualities," the other two being *rajas* (q.v.) and *tamas* (q.v.). Sattva is the quality of truth, goodness, reality, purity. These three guṇas or qualities run all through the web or fabric of nature like threads inextricably mingled, for, indeed, each of these three qualities participates likewise of the nature of the other two, yet each one possessing its predominant (which is its own svabhāva) or intrinsic characteristic. One who desires to gain some genuine understanding of the manner in which the archaic wisdom looks upon these three phases of human intellectual and spiritual activity must remember that not one of these three can be considered apart from the other two. The three are fundamentally three operations of the human consciousness, and essentially are that consciousness itself.

Science An operation of the human spirit-mind in its endeavor to understand the *how* of things — not any particular science whatsoever, but the thing in itself, science per se — ordered and classified knowledge. One phase of a triform method of understanding the nature of universal nature and its multiform and multifold workings; and this phase cannot be separated from the other two — philosophy (q.v.) and religion (q.v.) — if we wish to gain a true picture of things *as they are in themselves.*

Science is the aspect of human thinking in the activity of the mentality in the latter's inquisitive, researching, and classifying functions.

Second Death This is a phrase used by ancient and modern mystics to describe the dissolution of the principles of man remaining in kāma-loka after the death of the physical body. For instance, Plutarch says: "Of the deaths we die, the one makes man two of three, and the other, one out of two." Thus, using the simple division of man into spirit, soul, and body: the first death is the dropping of the body, making two out of three; the second death is the withdrawal of the spiritual from the kāma-rūpic soul, making one out of two.

The second death takes place when the lower or intermediate duad (manas-kāma) in its turn separates from, or rather is cast off by, the upper duad; but preceding this event the upper duad gathers unto itself from this lower duad what is called the reincarnating ego (q.v.), which is all the best of the entity that was, all its purest and most spiritual and noblest aspirations and hopes and dreams for betterment and for beauty and harmony. Inherent in the fabric, so to speak, of the reincarnating ego, there remain of course the seeds of the lower principles which at the succeeding rebirth or reincarnation of the ego will develop into the complex of the lower quaternary. (*See also* Kāma-Rūpa)

Self Man is a sheaf or bundle of forces or energies and material elements combined; and the power controlling all and holding them together, making out of the composite aggregate a unity, is what theosophists call the Self — not the mere ego, but the Self, a purely spiritual unit, in its essence divine, which is the same in every man and woman on earth, the same in every entity everywhere in all the boundless fields of limitless space, as we understand space. If one closely examine his own consciousness, he will very soon know that this is the pure consciousness expressed in the words, "I am" — and this is the Self; whereas the ego is the cognition of the "I am *I*."

Consider the hierarchy of the human being growing from the Self as its seed — ten stages: three on the arūpa or immaterial plane; and seven (or perhaps better, six) on the planes of matter or manifestation. On each one of these seven planes (or six planes), the Self or paramātman (q.v.) develops a sheath or garment, the upper ones spun of spirit, or light if you will, and the lower ones spun of shadow or matter; and each such sheath or garment is a soul; and between the Self and a soul — any soul — is an ego.

Seven Principles of Man Every one of the seven principles of man, as also every one of the seven elements in him, is itself a mirror of the universe. (*See* Principles of Man)

Seven Sacred Planets The ancients spoke of seven planets which they called the seven sacred planets, and they were named as follows: Saturn, Jupiter, Mars, Sun, Venus, Mercury, and Moon.

Each one of these seven globes is a body like our own Earth in that each is a septenary chain, sevenfold in composition: six other superior globes of finer and more ethereal matter above the physical sphere or globe. Only those globes which are on the same cosmic plane of nature or being are physically visible to each other. For instance, we can see only the fourth-plane planetary globe of each of the other planetary or sidereal chains, because we ourselves are on the fourth cosmic plane, as they also are. There is a very important and wide range of mystical teaching connected with the seven sacred planets which it would be out of place to develop here.

Shadows *See* Brothers of the Shadow

Shadowy Arc or **Descending Arc** *See* Ascending Arc

Silent Watcher A term used in modern theosophical esoteric philosophy to signify a highly advanced spiritual entity who is, as it were, the summit or supreme chief of a spiritual-psychological hierarchy composed of beings beneath him and working under the Silent Watcher's direct inspiration and guidance.

The Silent Watchers, therefore, are relatively numerous, because every hierarchy, large or small, high or low, has as its own particular hierarch or supreme head a Silent Watcher. There are human Silent Watchers, and there is a Silent Watcher for every globe of our planetary chain. There is likewise a Silent Watcher of the solar system of vastly loftier state or stage, etc.

"Silent Watcher" is a graphic phrase, and describes with fair accuracy the predominant trait or characteristic of such a spiritual being — one who through evolution having practically gained omniscience or perfect knowledge of all that he can learn in any one sphere of the kosmos, instead of pursuing his evolutionary path forwards to still higher realms, remains in order to help the multitudes and hosts of less progressed entities trailing behind him. There he remains at his self-imposed task, waiting and watching and helping and inspiring, and so far as we humans are concerned, in the utter silences of spiritual compassion. Thence the term Silent Watcher. He can learn nothing more from the particular sphere of life through which he has now passed, and the secrets of which he knows by heart. For the time being and for ages he has renounced all individual evolution for himself out of pure pity and high compassion for those beneath him.

Śishṭa(s) (*Śiṣṭa*, Sanskrit) This is a word meaning "remainders," or "remains," or "residuals" — anything that is left or remains behind. In the especial application in which this word is used in the ancient wisdom, the śishṭas are those superior classes — each of its own kind and kingdom — left behind on a planet when it goes into obscuration, in order to serve as the *seeds of life* for the inflow of the next incoming life-wave when the dawn of the new manvantara takes place on that planet.

When each kingdom passes on to its next globe, each one leaves behind its śishṭas, its lives representing the very highest point of evolution arrived at by that kingdom in that round, but leaves them sleeping as it were: dormant, relatively motionless, including life-atoms among them. Not without life, however, for everything is as much alive as ever, and there is no "dead" matter anywhere; but the śishṭas considered aggregatively as the remnants or residuals of the life-wave which has passed on are sleeping, dormant, resting. These śishṭas await the incoming of the life-waves on the next round, and then they re-awaken to a new cycle of activity as the seeds of the new kingdom or kingdoms — be it the three elemental kingdoms or the mineral or vegetable or the beast or the next humanity.

In a more restricted and still more specific sense, the śishṭas are the great elect, or sages, left behind after every obscuration.

Skandha(s) (Sanskrit) Literally "bundles," or groups of attributes, to use H. P. Blavatsky's definition. When death comes to a man in any one life, the seeds of those causes previously sown by him and which have not yet come forth into blossom and full-blown flower and fruit, remain in his interior and invisible parts as impulses lying latent and sleeping: lying latent like sleeping seeds for future flowerings into action in the next and succeeding lives. They are psychological impulse-seeds lying asleep until their appropriate stage for awakening into action arrives at some time in the future.

In the case of the cosmic bodies, every solar or planetary body upon entering into its pralaya, its prākṛitika-pralaya — the dissolution of its lower principles — at the end of its long life cycle, exists in space in the higher activity of its spiritual principles, and in the dispersion of its lowest principles, which latter latently exist in space as skandhas in a laya-condition.

When a laya-center (q.v.) is fired into action by the touch of wills and consciousnesses on their downward way, becoming the imbodying life of a solar system, or of a planet of a solar system, the center manifests first on its highest plane, and later on its lower plane. The skandhas are awakened into life one after another: first the highest ones, next the intermediate ones, and lastly the inferior ones, cosmically and qualitatively speaking.

The term skandhas in theosophical philosophy has the general significance of bundles or groups of attributes, which together form or compose the entire set of material and also mental, emotional, and moral qualities. Exoterically the skandhas are "bundles" of attributes five in number, but esoterically they are seven. These unite at the birth of man and constitute his personality. After the death of the body the skandhas are separated and so remain until the reincarnating ego (q.v.) on its downward path into physical incarnation gathers them together again around itself, and thus reforms the human constitution considered as a unity.

In brief, the skandhas can be said to be the aggregate of the groups of attributes or qualities which make each individual man the *personality* that he is; but this must be sharply distinguished from the individuality (q.v.).

Śloka (Sanskrit) "The Sanskrit epic meter formed of thirty-two syllables: verses in four half lines of eight, or in two lines of sixteen syllables each" (H. P. Blavatsky, *Theosophical Glossary*).

Soul This word in the ancient wisdom signifies "vehicle," and *upādhi* — that vehicle, or any vehicle, in which the monad, in any sphere of manifestation, is working out its destiny. A soul is an entity which is evolved by experiences; it is not a spirit, but it is a vehicle of a spirit — the monad. It manifests in matter through and by being a substantial portion of the lower essence of the spirit. Touching another plane below it, or it may be above it, the point of union allowing ingress and egress to the consciousness, is a laya-center — the neutral center, in matter or substance, through which consciousness passes — and the center of that consciousness is the monad. The soul in contradistinction with the monad is its vehicle for manifestation on any one plane. The spirit or monad manifests in seven vehicles, and each one of these vehicles is a soul.

On the higher planes the soul is a vehicle manifesting as a sheaf or pillar of light; similarly with the various egos and their related vehicle-souls on the inferior planes, all growing constantly more dense, as the planes of matter gradually thicken downwards and become more compact, into which the monadic ray penetrates until the final soul, which is the physical body, the general vehicle or bearer or carrier of them all.

Our teachings give to every animate thing a soul — not a human soul, or a divine soul, or a spiritual soul — but a soul corresponding to its own type. What it is, what its type is, actually comes from its soul; hence we properly may speak of the different beasts as having one or the other, a "duck soul," an "ostrich soul," a "bull" or a "cow soul," and so forth. The entities lower than man — in this case the beasts, considered as a kingdom, are differentiated into the different families of animals by the different souls within each. Of course behind the soul from which it springs there are in each individual entity all the other principles that likewise inform man; but all these higher principles are latent in the beast.

Speaking generally, however, we may say that the soul is the intermediate part between the spirit which is deathless and immortal on the one hand and, on the other hand, the physical frame, entirely mortal. The soul, therefore, is the intermediate part of the human constitution. It must be carefully noted in this connection that soul as a term employed in the esoteric philosophy, while indeed meaning essentially a "vehicle" or "sheath," this vehicle or sheath is nevertheless an animate or living entity much after the manner that the physical body, while being the sheath or vehicle of the other parts of man's constitution, is nevertheless in itself a discrete, animate, personalized being. (*See also* VĀHANA)

Soulless Beings "We elbow soulless men in the streets at every turn," wrote H. P. Blavatsky. This is an actual fact. The statement does not mean that those whom we thus elbow have no soul. The significance is that the spiritual part of these human beings is sleeping, not awake. They are animate humans with an animate working brain-mind, an animal mind, but otherwise "soulless" in the sense that the soul is inactive, sleeping; and this is also just what Pythagoras meant when he spoke of the "living dead." They are everywhere, these people. We elbow them, just as H. P. Blavatsky says, at every turn. The eyes may be physically bright, and filled with the vital physical fire, but they lack soul; they lack tenderness, the fervid yet gentle warmth of the living flame of inspiration within. Sometimes impersonal love will awaken the soul in a man or in a woman; sometimes it will kill it if the love become selfish and gross. The streets are filled with such "soulless" people; but the phrase soulless people does not mean "lost souls." The latter is again something else. The term soulless people therefore is a technical term. It means men and women who are still connected, but usually quite unconsciously, with the monad, the spiritual essence within them, but who are not *self-consciously* so connected. They live very largely in the brain-mind and in the fields of sensuous consciousness. They turn with pleasure to the frivolities of life. They have the ordinary feelings of honor, etc., because it is conventional and good breeding so to have them; but the deep inner fire of yearning, the living warmth that comes from being more or less at one with the god within, they know not. Hence, they are "soulless," because the soul is not working with fiery energy in and through them.

A lost soul, on the other hand, means an entity who through various rebirths, it may be a dozen, or more or less, has been slowly following the "easy descent to Avernus," and in whom the threads of communication with the spirit within have been snapped one after the other. Vice will do this, continuous vice. Hate snaps these spiritual threads more quickly than anything else perhaps. Selfishness, the parent of hate, is the root of all human evil; and therefore a lost soul is one who is not merely soulless in the ordinary theosophical usage of the word, but is one who has lost the last link, the last delicate thread of consciousness, connecting him with his inner god. He will continue "the easy descent," passing from human birth to an inferior human birth, and then to one still more inferior, until finally the degenerate astral monad — all that remains of the human being that once was — may even enter the body of some beast to which it feels attracted (and this is one side of the teaching of transmigration, which has been so badly misunderstood in the Occident); some finally go even to plants perhaps, at the last, and will ultimately vanish. The astral monad will then have faded out. Such lost souls are exceedingly rare, fortunately; but they are not what we call soulless people.

If the student will remember the fact that when a human being is filled with the living spiritual and intellectual fiery energies flowing into his brain-mind from his inner god, he is then an insouled being, he will readily understand that when these fiery energies can no longer reach the brain-mind and manifest in a man's life, there is thus produced what is called a soulless being. A good man, honorable, loyal, compassionate, aspiring, gentle, and true-hearted, and a student of wisdom, is an "insouled" man; a buddha is one who is fully, completely insouled; and there are all the intermediate grades between.

Space Our universe, as popularly supposed, consists of space and matter and energy; but in theosophy we say that space itself is both conscious and substantial. It is in fact the root of the other two, matter and energy, which are fundamentally one thing, and this one fundamental thing is SPACE — their essential and also their instrumental cause as well as their substantial cause — and this is the reality of being, the heart of things.

Our teaching is that there are many universes, not merely one, our own home-universe; therefore are there many spaces with a background of a perfectly incomprehensible greater SPACE inclosing all — a space which is still more ethereal, tenuous, spiritual, yes, divine, than the space-matter that we know or rather conceive of, which in its lowest aspect manifests the grossness of physical matter of common human knowledge. Space, therefore, considered in the abstract, is BEING, filled full, so to say, with other entities and things, of which we see a small part — globes innumerable, stars and planets, nebulae and comets.

But all these material bodies are but effectual products or results of the infinitudes of the invisible and inner causal realms — by far the larger part of the spaces of Space. The space therefore of any one universe is an entity — a god. Fundamentally and essentially it is a spiritual entity, a divine entity indeed, of which we see naught but what we humans call the material and energic aspect — behind which is the causal life, the causal intelligence.

The word is likewise frequently used in theosophical philosophy to signify the frontierless infinitudes of the Boundless; and because it is the very *esse* of life-consciousness-substance, it is incomparably more than the mere "container" that it is so often supposed to be by Occidental philosophers. (*See also* Universe, Milky Way)

Spirit In the theosophical philosophy there is a distinct and important difference in the use of the words *spirit* and *soul.* The spirit is the immortal element in us, the deathless flame within us which dies never, which never was born and which retains throughout the entire mahā-manvantara its own quality, essence, and life, sending down into our own being and into our various planes certain of its rays or garments or souls *which we are.*

The divine spirit of man is linked with the All, being in a highly mystical sense a ray of the All.

A soul is an entity which is evolved by experiences; it is not a spirit because it is a vehicle of a spirit. It manifests in matter through and by being a substantial portion of the lower essence of the spirit. Touching another plane below it, or it may be above it, the point of union allowing ingress and egress to the consciousness is a laya-center. The spirit manifests in seven vehicles, and each one of these vehicles is a soul; and that particular point through which the spiritual influence passes in the soul is the laya-center, the heart of the soul, or rather the summit thereof — homogeneous soul-substance, if you like.

In a kosmical sense spirit should be applied only to that which belongs without qualifications to universal consciousness and which is the homogeneous and unmixed emanation from the universal consciousness. In the case of man, the spirit within man is the flame of his deathless ego, the direct emanation of the spiritual monad within him, and of this ego the spiritual soul is the enclosing sheath or vehicle or garment. Making an application more particularly and specifically to the human principles, when the higher manas of man which is his real ego is indissolubly linked with buddhi, this, in fact, is the spiritual ego or spirit of the individual human being's constitution. Its life term before the emanation is withdrawn into the divine monad is for the full period of a kosmic manvantara.

Spirit (in reference to Matter) The theosophist points out that what men call spirit is the summit or acme or root or seed or beginning or noumenon — call it by any name — of any particular hierarchy existing in the innumerable hosts of the kosmic hierarchies, with all of which any such hierarchy is inextricably interblended and interworking.

When theosophists speak of spirit and substance, of which matter and energy or force are the physicalized expressions, we must remember that all these terms are abstractions, generalized expressions for certain entities manifesting aggregatively.

Spirit, for instance, is not essentially different from matter, and is only relatively so different, or evolutionally so different: the difference not lying in the roots of these two where they become one in the underlying consciousness-reality, but in their characters they are two evolutional forms of manifestation of that underlying reality. In other words, to use the terminology of modern scientific philosophy, spirit and matter are, each of them, respectively an "event" as the underlying reality passes through eternal duration.

Spiritual Soul The spiritual soul is the vehicle of the individual monad, the jīvātman or spiritual ego; in the case of man's principles it is essentially of the nature of ātma-buddhi. This spiritual ego is the center or seed or root of the reincarnating ego. It is that portion of our spiritual constitution which is deathless as an individualized entity — deathless until the end of the mahā-manvantara of the cosmic solar system.

The spiritual soul and the divine soul, or ātman, combined, are the inner god — the inner buddha, the inner christ.

Sthūla-Śarīra (Sanskrit) *Sthūla* means "coarse," "gross," not refined, heavy, bulky, fat in the sense of bigness, therefore, conditioned and differentiated matter; *śarīra,* "form," generally speaking. The lowest substance-principle of which man is composed, usually classified as the seventh in order — the physical body.

The sthūla-śarīra or physical hierarchy of the human body is builded up of cosmic elements, themselves formed of living atomic entities which, although subject individually to bewilderingly rapid changes and reimbodiments, nevertheless are incomparably more enduring in themselves as expressions of the monadic rays than is the transitory physical body which they temporarily compose.

The physical body is composed mostly of porosity, if the expression be pardoned; the most *unreal* thing we know, full of holes, foamy as it were. At death the physical body follows the course of natural decay, and its various hosts of life-atoms proceed individually and collectively whither their natural attractions call them.

Strictly speaking, the physical body is not a principle at all; it is merely a house, man's carrier in another sense, and no more is an essential part of him — except that he has *excreted* it, *thrown it out from himself* — than are the clothes in which his body is garmented. Man really is a complete human being without the sthūla-śarīra; and yet this statement while accurate must be taken not too literally, because even the physical body is the expression of man's constitution on the physical plane. The meaning is that the human constitution can be a complete human entity even when the physical body is discarded, but the sthūla-śarīra is needed for evolution and active work on this subplane of the solar kosmos.

Śūdra (Sanskrit) In ancient India a man of the servile or fourth or lowest caste, social and political, of the early civilizations of Hindustan in the Vedic and post-Vedic periods. The other three grades or classes are respectively the *Brāhmaṇa* or priest-philosopher; the *Kshatriya,* the administrator — king, noble — and soldier; and third, the *Vaiśya,* the trader and agriculturist (see these three).

Sushupti *See* JĀGRAT, KĀRAṆOPĀDHI

Sūtrātman (Sanskrit) A compound word meaning "thread-self," the golden thread of individuality — the stream of self-consciousness — on which all the substance-principles of man's constitution are strung, so to say, like pearls on a golden chain. The sūtrātman is the stream of consciousness-life running through all the various substance-principles of the constitution of the human entity — or indeed of any other entity. Each such pearl on the golden chain is one of the countless personalities which man uses during the course of his manvantara-long evolutionary progress. The sūtrātman, therefore, may be briefly said to be the immortal or spiritual monadic ego, the individuality which incarnates in life after life, and therefore is rightly called the thread-self or fundamental self.

It is this sūtrātman, this thread-self, this consciousness-stream, or rather stream of consciousness-life, which is the fundamental and individual selfhood of every entity, and which, reflected in and through the several intermediate vehicles or veils or sheaths or garments of the invisible constitution of man, or of any other being in which a monad enshrouds itself, produces the egoic centers of self-conscious existence. The sūtrātman, therefore, is rooted in the monad, the monadic essence.

Svabhāva (Sanskrit) A compound word derived from the verb-root *bhū,* meaning "to become" — not so much "to be" in the passive sense, but rather "to become," to "grow into" something. The quasi-pronominal prefix *sva,* means "self"; hence the noun means "self-becoming," "self-generation," "self-growing" into something. Yet the essential or fundamental or integral *Self,* although following continuously its own lofty line of evolution, cannot be said to suffer the changes or phases that its vehicles undergo. Like the monads, like the One, thus the Self fundamental — which, after all, is virtually the same as the one monadic essence — sends down a ray from itself into every organic entity, much as the sun sends a ray from itself into the surrounding "darkness" of the solar universe.

Svabhāva has two general philosophical meanings: first, self-begetting, self-generation, self-becoming, the general idea being that there is no merely mechanical or soulless activity of nature in bringing us into being, for *we brought ourselves forth,* in and through and by nature, of which we are a part of the conscious forces, and therefore are our own children. The second meaning is that each and every entity that exists is the result of what he actually is spiritually in his own higher nature: he brings forth *that which he is in himself interiorly,* nothing else. A particular race, for instance, remains and is that race as long as the particular race-svabhāva remains in the racial seed and manifests thus. Likewise is the case the same with a man, a tree, a star, a god — what not!

What makes a rose bring forth a rose always and not thistles or daisies or pansies? The answer is very simple; very profound, however. It is because of its svabhāva, the essential nature in and of the seed. Its svabhāva can bring forth only that which itself is, its essential characteristic, its own inner nature. Svabhāva, in short, may be called the essential individuality of any monad, expressing its own characteristics, qualities, and type, by *self-urged evolution.*

The seed can produce nothing but what it itself is, what is in it; and this is the heart and essence of the doctrine of svabhāva. The philosophical, scientific, and religious reach of this doctrine is simply immense; and it is of the first importance. Consequently, each individual svabhāva brings forth and expresses as its own particular vehicles its various *svarūpas,* signifying characteristic bodies or images or forms. The svabhāva of a dog, for instance, brings forth the dog body. The svabhāva of a rose brings forth the rose flower; the svabhāva of a man brings forth man's shape or image;

and the svabhāva of a divinity or god brings forth its own *svarūpa* or characteristic vehicle.

Svabhavat (Sanskrit) The neuter present participle of a compound word derived from the verb-root *bhū,* meaning "to become," from which is derived a secondary meaning "to be," in the sense of growth.

Svabhavat is a state or condition of cosmic consciousness-substance, where spirit and matter, which are fundamentally one, no longer are dual as in manifestation, but one: that which is neither manifested matter nor manifested spirit alone, but both are the primeval unity — spiritual ākāśa — where matter merges into spirit, and both now being really one, are called "Father-Mother," spirit-substance. Svabhavat never descends from its own state or condition, or from its own plane, but is the cosmic reservoir of being, as well as of beings, therefore of consciousness, of intellectual light, of life; and it is the ultimate source of what science, in our day, so quaintly calls the energies of nature universal.

The northern Buddhists call svabhavat by a more mystical term, Ādi-buddhi, "primeval buddhi"; the Brahmanical scriptures call it ākāśa; and the Hebrew Old Testament refers to it as the cosmic "waters."

The difference in meaning between svabhavat and svabhāva (q.v.) is very great and is not generally understood; the two words often have been confused. Svabhāva is the characteristic nature, the type-essence, the individuality, of svabhavat — of any svabhavat, each such svabhavat having its own svabhāva. Svabhavat, therefore, is really the *world-substance* or stuff, or still more accurately that which is causal of the world-substance, and this causal principle or element is the spirit and essence of cosmic substance. It is the plastic *essence* of matter, both manifest and unmanifest. (*See also* ĀKĀŚA)

Svapna *See* JĀGRAT

Svarūpa *See* SVABHĀVA

— T —

Tala (Sanskrit) A word which is largely used in the metaphysical systems of India, both in contrast and at the same time in conjunction with loka (q.v.). As the general meaning of loka is "place" or rather "world," so the general meaning of tala is "inferior world." Every loka has as its twin or counterpart a corresponding tala. Wherever there is a loka there is an exactly correspondential tala, and in fact the tala is the nether pole of its corresponding loka. Lokas and talas, therefore, in a way of speaking, may be considered to be the spiritual and the material aspects or substance-principles of the different worlds which compose and in fact are the kosmic universe. It is impossible to separate a tala from its corresponding loka — quite as impossible as it would be to separate the two poles of electricity.

The number of talas as generally outlined in the exoteric philosophies of Hindustan is usually given as seven, there being thus seven lokas and seven talas; but, as a matter of fact, this number varies. If we may speak of a loka as the spiritual pole, we may likewise call it the principle of any world; and correspondentially when we speak of the tala as being the negative or inferior pole, it is quite proper also to refer to it as the element of its corresponding loka or principle. Hence, the lokas of a hierarchy may be called the principles of a hierarchy, and the talas, in exactly the same way, may be called the elements or substantial or material aspects of the hierarchy.

It should likewise be remembered that all the seven lokas and all the seven talas are continuously and inextricably interblended and interworking; and that the lokas and the talas working together form the universe and its various subordinate hierarchies that encompass us around. The higher lokas with the higher talas are the forces or energies and substantial parts of the spiritual and ethereal worlds; the lowest lokas and their corresponding talas form the forces or energies and substantial parts of the physical world surrounding us; and the intermediate lokas with their corresponding talas form the respective energies and substantial parts of the intermediate or ethereal realms.

Briefly, therefore, we may speak of a tala as the material aspect of the world where it predominates, just as when speaking of a loka we may consider it to be the spiritual aspect of the world where it predominates. Every loka, it should be always remembered, is coexistent with and cannot be separated from its corresponding tala on the same plane.

As an important deduction from the preceding observations, be it carefully noted that man's own constitution as an individual from the highest to the lowest is a hierarchy of its own kind, and therefore man himself as such a subordinate hierarchy is a composite entity formed of lokas and talas inextricably interworking and intermingled. In this subordinate hierarchy called man live and evolve vast armies, hosts, multitudes, of living entities, monads in this inferior stage of their long evolutionary peregrination, and which for convenience and brevity of expression we may class under the general term of life-atoms (q.v.).

Tamas (Sanskrit) One of the three guṇas or qualities or essential attributes of manifested beings and things. Tamas is the quality of darkness, illusion, ignorance; it also means, in a quite different sense, quiescence, passivity, repose, rest, inertia. It becomes immediately obvious from the distinctions that these two series of words show, that there is both a good and an evil side to tamas, just as indeed there is a good and evil side to rajas (q.v.), and even to sattva (q.v.). The condition of manifested existence in the state of cosmic pralaya is in one sense of the word the tāmasic condition, signifying quiescence or rest. When the universe is in the stage of active manvantaric manifestation, we may in a generalizing sense say that the universe is in the rājasic state or condition; and that aspect of the universe which we may call the divine-spiritual, whether in the universe itself or in the manvantara or in the pralaya of a globe, can be spoken of as the sāttvic state or condition. From these observations it should be evident that the three guṇas — sattva, rajas, tamas — not only can exist contemporaneously and coincidently, but actually do so exist, and that in fact the three are inextricably interblended. They are really three phases or conditions of imbodied consciousnesses, and each has its noble and each its "evil" side.

Tanhā (Pāli) A word familiar in Buddhism and signifying the "thirst" for material life. It is this thirst or yearning to return to familiar scenes that brings the reincarnating ego (q.v.) back to earth-life — and this yearning is more effectual as an individual cause for reincarnation, perhaps, than all else. (*See also* TṚISHṆĀ)

Tantra(s) (Sanskrit) A word literally meaning a "loom" or the warp or threads in a loom, and, by extension of meaning, signifying a rule or ritual for ceremonial rites. The Hindu Tantras are numerous works or religious treatises teaching mystical and magical formulae or formularies for the attainment of magical or quasi-magical powers, and for the worship of the gods. They are mostly composed in the form of dialogs between Śiva and his divine consort Durgā, these two divinities being the peculiar objects of the adoration of the Tāntrins.

In many parts of India the authority of the Tantras seems almost to have superseded the clean and poetical hymns of the Vedas.

Most tantric works are supposed to contain five different subjects: (1) the manifestation or evolution of the universe; (2) its destruction; (3) the worship or adoration of the divinities; (4) the achievement or attainment of desired objects and especially of six superhuman faculties; (5) modes or methods of union, usually enumerated as four, with the supreme divinity of the kosmos by means of contemplative meditation.

Unfortunately, while there is much of interest in the tantric works, their tendency for long ages has been distinctly towards what in occultism is known as sorcery or black magic. Some of the rites or ceremonies practiced have to do with revolting details connected with sex.

Durgā, the consort of Śiva, his śakti or energy, is worshiped by the Tāntrins as a distinct personified female power.

The origin of the Tantras unquestionably goes back to a very remote antiquity, and there seems to be little doubt that these works, or their originals, were heirlooms handed down from originally debased or degenerate Atlantean racial offshoots. There is, of course, a certain amount of profoundly philosophical and mystical thought running through the more important tantric works, but the tantric worship in many cases is highly licentious and immoral.

Tāntrik or **Tāntrika** (Sanskrit) The adjective corresponding to tantra (q.v.). This adjective, however, is sometimes employed to signify one who is deeply versed in some study — a scholar; but more particularly the adjective concerns the Tantras and the doctrines contained in them.

Tat (Sanskrit) A pronominal neuter particle which is often used as a noun having the signification THAT. By this word the Vedic sages and archaic scriptural writers of India described the unutterable principle from which all in a single kosmic universe sprang, contrasting it with the pronominal particle *idam,* meaning "this" and signifying the manifested universe. (*See also* PARABRAHMAN)

Tattvas (Sanskrit) A word the meaning of which is the elementary principles or elements of original substance, or rather the different principles or elements in universal, intelligent, conscious nature when considered from the standpoint of occultism. The word tattva perhaps may be literally translated or rendered as "thatness," reminding one of the "quiddity" of the European Scholastics.

The number of tattvas or nature's elemental principles varies according to different systems of philosophy. The Sānkhya, for instance, enumerates twenty-five tattvas. The system of the Māheśvaras or worshipers of Śiva with his consort Durgā, reckons five principles, which are simply the five elements of nature found in all ancient literatures. Occultism, of course, recognizes seven tattvas, and, indeed, ten fundamental element-principles or element-substances or tattvas in universal nature, and each one of these tattvas is represented in the human constitution and active therein. Otherwise, the human constitution could not cohere as an organic entity.

That *See* Parabrahman, Tat

Theosophy A compound Greek word: *theos,* a "divine being," a "god"; *sophia,* "wisdom"; hence divine wisdom. Theosophy is the majestic wisdom-religion of the archaic ages and is as old as thinking man. It was delivered to the first human protoplasts, the first thinking human beings on this earth, by highly intelligent spiritual entities from superior spheres. This ancient doctrine, this esoteric system, has been passed down from guardians to guardians to guardians through innumerable generations until our own time. Furthermore, portions of this original and majestic system have been given out at various periods of time to various races in various parts of the world by those guardians when humanity stood in need of such extension and elaboration of spiritual and intellectual thought.

Theosophy is not a syncretistic philosophy-religion-science, a system of thought or belief which has been put together piecemeal and consisting of parts or portions taken by some great mind from other various religions or philosophies. This idea is false. On the contrary, theosophy is that single system or systematic formulation of the facts of visible and invisible nature which, as expressed through the illuminated human mind, takes the apparently separate forms of science and of philosophy and of religion. We may likewise describe theosophy to be the formulation in human language of the nature, structure, origin, destiny, and operations of the kosmical universe and of the multitudes of beings which infill it.

It might be added that theosophy, in the language of H. P. Blavatsky (*Theosophical Glossary,* p. 328), is "the sub-stratum and basis of all the world-religions and philosophies, taught and practiced by a few elect ever since man became a thinking being. In its practical bearing, Theosophy is purely *divine ethics*; the definitions in dictionaries are pure nonsense, based on religious prejudice and ignorance." (*See also* Universal Brotherhood)

Thought Transference The power of transferring one's thoughts without a word — voiceless speech. This is no psychical power. Its psychical aspect, commonly called thought transference or telepathy, is but a feeble manifestation of a truly sublime power, and is illusory, because it is but a reflected light of the real spiritual power within. True thought transference is a spiritual faculty. Having this spiritual power you can transfer your thought and your consciousness and your will to any part of the earth — and actually be there, see what goes on, know what is happening there. No merely psychical power will ever enable you to do that. In Tibet this power is called by the generalizing name hpho-wa. Having this power your conscious and percipient inner self can pass through stone walls as easily as the electric current runs along or through the copper wire. (*See also* Māyāvi-Rūpa)

Transmigration This word is grossly misunderstood in the modern Occident, as also is the doctrine comprised under the old Greek word metempsychosis, both being modernly supposed to mean, through the common misunderstanding of the ancient literatures, that the human soul at some time after death migrates into the beast realm and is reborn on earth in a beast body. The real meaning of this statement in ancient literature refers to the destiny of what theosophists call the life-atoms (q.v.), but it has absolutely no reference to the destiny of the *human* soul, as an entity.

Theosophy accepts all aspects of the ancient teaching, but explains and interprets them. Our doctrine in this respect unless, indeed, we are treating of the case of a "lost soul" (q.v.), is "once a man, always a man." The human soul can no more migrate over and incarnate in a beast body than can the psychical apparatus of a beast incarnate in human flesh. Why? Because in the former case, the beast vehicle offers to the human soul no opening at all for the expression of the spiritual and intellectual and psychical powers and faculties and tendencies which make a man human. Nor can the soul of the beast enter into a human body, because the impassable gulf of a psychical and intellectual nature, which separates the two kingdoms, prevents any such passage from the one up into another so much its superior in all respects. In the former case, there is no attraction for the man beastwards; and in the latter case there is the impossibility of the imperfectly developed beast mind and beast soul finding a proper lodgment in what to it is truly a godlike sphere which it simply cannot enter.

Transmigration, however, has a specific meaning when the word is applied to the human soul: the living entity migrates or passes over from one condition to another condition or state or plane, as the case may be, whether these latter be in the invisible realms of nature or in the visible realms, and whether the state or condition be high or low. The specific meaning of this word, therefore, implies nothing more than a change of state or of condition or of plane: a migrating of the living entity from one to the other, but always in conditions or estates or habitudes appropriate and pertaining to its human dignity.

In its application to the life-atoms, to which are to be referred the observations of the ancients with regard to the lower realms of nature, transmigration means briefly that the particular life-atoms, which in their aggregate compose man's lower principles, at and following the change that men call death migrate or transmigrate or pass into other bodies to which these life-atoms are attracted by similarity of development — be these attractions high or low, and they are usually low, because their own evolutionary development is as a rule far from being advanced. Nevertheless, it should be remembered that these life-atoms compose man's inner — and outer — vehicles or bodies, and that in consequence there are various grades or classes of these life-atoms, from the physical upwards (or inwards if you please) to the astral, purely vital, emotional, mental, and psychical.

This is, in general terms, the meaning of transmigration. The word means no more than the specific senses just outlined, and stops there. But the teaching concerning the destiny of the entity is continued and developed in the doctrine pertaining to the word metempsychosis (q.v.).

Tretā Yuga *See* YUGA

Tṛishṇā (Sanskrit) The meaning of this word is "thirst" or "longing," but it is a technical term imbodying the idea that it is this "thirst" for the things which the human ego formerly knew, and which it wills and desires to know again — things familiar and akin to it from past experiences — which draws the intermediate nature or human ego of man back again to incarnation in earth-life. It is attracted anew to what is to it old and familiar worlds and scenes; it thirsts for the manifested life comprising them, for the things which it formerly made akin to itself; and thus is it attracted back to those spheres which it left at some preceding period of its evolutionary journey through them, when death overtook it. Its attraction to return to earth is naught but an operation of a law of nature. Here the intermediate nature or human ego sowed the seeds of thought and of action in past lives, and here therefore must it of necessity reap their fruits. It cannot reap where it has not sown, as is obvious enough. It never goes whither it is not attracted or drawn.

After death has released the intermediate nature, and during long ages has given to it its period of bliss and rest and psychical recuperation — much as a quiet and reposeful night's sleep is to the tired physical body — then, just as a man reawakens by degrees, so does this intermediate nature or human ego by degrees recede or awaken from that state of rest and bliss called devachan (q.v.). And the seeds of thoughts, the seeds of actions which it had done in former lives, are now laid by in the fabric of itself — seeds whose natural energy is still unexpended and unexhausted — and inhere in that inner psychical fabric, for they have nowhere else in which to inhere, since the man produced them there and they are a part of him. These seeds of former thoughts and acts, of former emotions, desires, loves, hates, yearnings, and aspirations, each one of such begins to make itself felt as an urge earthwards, towards the spheres and planes in which they are native, and where they naturally grow and expand and develop.

In this our present life, all of us are setting in motion causes in thought and in action which will bring us back to this earth in the distant future. We shall then reap the harvest of the seeds of thought and action that we are in this present life planting in the fields of our human nature.

In the Pāli books of the Orient this word is called tanhā (q.v.).

Turīya *See* Jāgrat, Kāraṇopādhi

— U —

Universal Brotherhood Universal brotherhood as understood in the esoteric philosophy, and which is a sublime natural fact of universal nature, does not signify merely sentimental unity, or a simple political or social cooperation. Its meaning is incomparably wider and profounder than this. The sense inherent in the words in their widest tenor or purport is the *spiritual brotherhood of all beings*; particularly, the doctrine implies that all human beings are inseparably linked together, not merely by the bonds of emotional thought or feeling, but by the very fabric of the universe itself, all men — as well as all beings, both high and low and intermediate — springing forth from the inner and spiritual sun of the universe as its hosts of spiritual rays. We all come from this one source, that spiritual sun, and are all builded of the same life-atoms on all the various planes.

It is this interior unity of being and of consciousness, as well as the exterior union of us all, which enables us to grasp intellectually and spiritually the mysteries of the universe; because not merely ourselves and our own fellow human beings, but also all other beings and things that are, are children of the same kosmic parent, great Mother Nature, in all her seven (and ten) planes or worlds of being. We are all rooted in the same kosmic essence, whence we all proceeded in the beginning of the primordial periods of world evolution, and towards which we are all journeying back. This interlocking and interblending of the numberless hierarchies of beings forming the universe itself extends everywhere, in the invisible worlds as well as in the worlds which are visible.

Finally, it is upon this fact of the spiritual unity of all beings and things that reposes the basis and foundation of human ethics when these last are properly understood. In the esoteric philosophy ethics are no mere human convention or rules of action convenient and suitable for the amelioration of the asperities of human intercourse, but are fundamental in the very structure and inextricably coordinated operations of the universe itself.

Universal Self The universal self is the heart of the universe, for these two phrases are but two manners of expressing the same thing. It is the source of our being; it is also the goal whither we are all marching, we and the hierarchies above us as well as the hierarchies and the entities which compose them inferior to us. All come from the same ineffable source, the heart of being, the universal self. All pass at one period of their evolutionary journey through the stage of humanity, gaining thereby self-consciousness or the ego-self, the "I am I," and they find this ego-self or consciousness, as they advance along this evolutionary path, expanding gradually into universal consciousness — an expansion, however, which never has an end, because the universal consciousness is endless, limitless, boundless, and without any frontiers whatsoever. (*See also* Paramātman, Self)

Universe The theosophical philosophy divides the universe into two general functional portions — one the consciousness side, the abode or dwelling place, and at the same time the aggregate, of all the self-conscious, thinking entities that the boundless universe contains; and the other, the material side of nature, which is their schoolhouse, their home, and their playground too. This so-called material side is a practically infinite aggregate of monads or consciousness-centers passing through that particular phase of their evolutionary journey.

This universe, therefore, is a vast aggregate of consciousness-centers in both the two functional portions of it; and these consciousness-centers theosophists call monads. They are entities conscious in differing degrees, stretching along the boundless scale of the universal life; but in that particular phase which passes through what we humans call matter, those monads belonging to and forming that side of the universe, in the course of their long, long, evolutionary journey have not yet attained self-conscious powers or faculties. And furthermore, what we call matter, in its last analysis is actually an aggregate of these monads manifesting in their physical expressions as life-atoms.

The consciousness side of universal nature, which also consists of countless hosts of self-conscious entities, works in and through this other or material side; for these hosts of consciousnesses self-express themselves through this other or material function or side, through these other countless hosts of younger and inferior and embryo entities, which are the life-atoms — embryo gods. The universe is therefore actually and literally imbodied consciousnesses.

Upādhi (Sanskrit) A word which is used in various senses in Indian philosophy, the vocable itself meaning "limitation" or "a peculiarity" and hence "a disguise"; and from this last meaning arises the expression "vehicle," which it often bears in modern theosophical philosophy. The gist of the word signifies "that which stands forth following a model or pattern," as a canvas, so to say, upon which the light from a projecting lantern plays. An upādhi therefore, mystically speaking, is like a play of shadow and form, when compared with the ultimate reality, which is the cause of this play of shadow and form. Man may be considered as a being composed of three (or even four) essential upādhis or bases.

Upanishad (Sanskrit) A compound, composed of *upa* "according to," "together with," *ni* "down," and the verbal root *sad,* "to sit," which becomes *shad* by Sanskrit grammar when preceded by the particle *ni*: the entire compound thus signifying "following upon or according to the teachings which were received when we were sitting down." The figure here is that of pupils sitting in the Oriental style at the feet of the teacher, who taught them the secret wisdom or rahasya, in private and in forms and manners of expression that later were written and promulgated according to those teachings and after that style.

The Upanishads are examples of literary works in which the rahasya — a Sanskrit word meaning "esoteric doctrine" or "mystery" — is imbodied. The Upanishads belong to the Vedic cycle and are regarded by orthodox Brahmans as a portion of the *śruti* or "revelation." It was from these wonderful quasi-esoteric and very mystical works that was later developed the highly philosophical and profound system called the Vedānta. The Upanishads are usually reckoned today as one hundred and fifty in number, though probably only a score are now complete without evident marks of literary change or adulteration in the way of excision or interpolation.

The topics treated of in the Upanishads are highly transcendental, recondite, and abstruse, and in order properly to understand the Upanishadic teaching one should have constantly in mind the master-keys that theosophy puts into the hand of the student. The origin of the universe, the nature of the divinities, the relations between soul and ego, the connections of spiritual and material beings, the liberation of the evolving entity from the chains of māyā, and kosmological questions, are all dealt with, mostly in a succinct and cryptic form. The Upanishads, finally, may be called the exoteric theosophical works of Hindustan, but contain a vast amount of genuine esoteric information.

— V —

Vāch (Sanskrit) A term which means "speech" or "word"; and by the same procedure of mystical thought which is seen in ancient Greek mysticism, wherein the Logos is not merely the speech or word of the Divinity, but also the divine reason, so Vāch has come to mean really more than merely word or speech. The esoteric Vāch is the subjective creative intelligent force which, emanating from the subjective universe, becomes the manifested or concrete expression of ideation, hence Word or Logos. Mystically, therefore, Vāch may be said to be the feminine or vehicular aspect of the Logos, or the power of the Logos when enshrined within its vehicle or sheath of action. Vāch in India is often called *Śata-rūpā,* "the hundred-formed." Cosmologically in one sense daivīprakṛiti (q.v.) may be said to be a manifestation or form of Vāch.

Vāhana (Sanskrit) A "vehicle" or carrier. This word has a rather wide currency in philosophical and esoteric and occult thought. Its signification is a bearer or vehicle of some entity which, through this carrier or vehicle, is enabled to manifest itself on planes or in spheres or worlds hierarchically inferior to its own. Thus the vāhana of man is, generally speaking, his body, although indeed man's constitution comprises a number of vāhanas or vehicles, each one belonging to — and enabling the inner man, or manifesting spiritual or intellectual entity, to express itself on — the plane where the vāhana is native.

Vāhana is thus seen to have a number of different meanings, or, more accurately, applications. E.g., the vāhana of man's spiritual monad is his spiritual soul; the vāhana of man's human ego is his human soul; and the vāhana of man's psycho-vital-astral monad is the liṅga-śarīra working through its vāhana or carrier, the sthūla-śarīra or physical body. The wire which carries the current of electricity can be said to be the vāhana of the electric current; or again, the intermolecular ether is the vāhana of many of the radioactive forces of the world around us, etc. Every divine being has a vāhana or, in fact, a number of vāhanas, through which it works and through which it is enabled to express its divine powers and functions on and in worlds and planes below the sphere or world or plane in which it itself lives. (*See also* SOUL, UPĀDHI)

Vaiśya (Sanskrit) The third of the four castes or social classes into which the inhabitants of ancient India were divided. The Vaiśya is the trader and agriculturist. (*See also* BRĀHMAṆA, KSHATRIYA, ŚŪDRA)

Vedānta (Sanskrit) From the Upanishads and from other parts of the wonderful cycle of Vedic literature, the ancient sages of India produced what is called today the Vedānta — a compound word meaning "the end (or completion) of the Veda" — that is to say, instruction in the final and most perfect exposition of the meaning of the Vedic tenets.

The Vedānta is the highest form that the Brahmanical teachings have taken, and under the name of the *Uttara-Mīmāṃsā* attributed to Vyāsa, the compiler of the Vedas, the Vedānta is perhaps the noblest of the six Indian schools of philosophy. The Avatāra Śaṅkarāchārya has been the main popularizer of the Vedāntic system of philosophical thought, and the type of Vedāntic doctrine taught by him is what is technically called the *Advaita-Vedānta* or nondualistic.

The Vedānta may briefly be described as a system of mystical philosophy derived from the efforts of sages through many generations to interpret the sacred or esoteric meaning of the Upanishads. In its *Advaita* form the Vedānta is in many, if not all, respects exceedingly close to, if not identical with, some of the mystical forms of Buddhism in central Asia. The Hindus call the Vedānta *Brahma-jñāna.*

Veda(s) (Sanskrit) From a verbal root *vid* signifying "to know." These are the most ancient and the most sacred literary and religious works of the Hindus. *Veda* as a word may be described as "divine knowledge." The Vedas are four in number: the *Ṛig-Veda,* the *Yajur-Veda,* the *Sāma-Veda,* and the *Atharva-Veda,* this last being commonly supposed to be of later date than the former three.

Manu in his *Work on Law* always speaks of the three Vedas, which he calls "the ancient triple Brahman" — *sanātanam trayam brahma.*" Connected with the Vedas is a large body of other works of various kinds, liturgical, ritualistic, exegetical, and mystical, the Veda itself being commonly divided into two great portions, outward and inner: the former called the *karma-kāṇḍa,* the "Section of Works," and the latter called *jñāna-kāṇḍa* or "Section of Wisdom."

The authorship of the Veda is not unitary, but almost every hymn or division of a Veda is ascribed to a different author or rather to various authors; but they are supposed to have been compiled in their present form by Veda-Vyāsa. There is no question in the minds of learned students of theosophy that the Vedas run back in their origins to enormous antiquity, thousands of years before the beginning of what is known in the Occident as the Christian era, whatever Occidental scholars may have to say in objection to this statement. Hindu pandits themselves claim that the Veda was taught orally for thousands of years, and then finally compiled on the shores of the sacred lake Mānasa-Sarovara, beyond the Himalayas in a district of what is now Tibet.

Vidyā (Sanskrit) The word (derived from the same verbal root *vid* from which comes the noun *Veda*) for "knowledge," "philosophy," "science." This is a term very generally used in theosophical philosophy, having in a general way the three meanings just stated. It is frequently compounded with other words, such as: *ātma-vidyā* — "knowledge of ātman" or the essential Self; *Brahma-vidyā* — "knowledge of Brahman," knowledge of the universe, a term virtually equivalent to theosophy; or, again, *guhya-vidyā* — signifying the "secret knowledge" or the esoteric wisdom. Using the word in a collective but nevertheless specific sense, vidyā is a general term for occult science.

— W —

White Magicians *See* BROTHERS OF THE SHADOW

— Y —

Yama *See* SAMĀDHI

Yoga (Sanskrit) Literally "union," "conjunction," etc. In India it is the technical name for one of the six Darśanas or schools of philosophy, and its foundation is ascribed to the sage Patañjali. The name Yoga itself describes the objective of this school, the attaining of union or at-one-ness with the divine-spiritual essence within a man. The yoga practices when properly understood through the instructions of genuine teachers — who, by the way, never announce themselves as public lecturers or through books or advertisements — are supposed to induce certain ecstatic states leading to a clear perception of universal truths, and the highest of these states is called samādhi (q.v.).

There are a number of minor forms of yoga practice and training such as the karma yoga, haṭha yoga, bhakti yoga, rāja yoga, jñāna yoga, etc. Similar religious aspirations or practices likewise exist in Occidental countries, as, for instance, what is called salvation by works, somewhat equivalent to the Hindu karma yoga or, again, salvation by faith — or love, somewhat similar to the Hindu bhakti yoga; while both Orient and Occident have, each one, its various forms of ascetic practices which may be grouped under the term haṭha yoga.

No system of yoga should ever be practiced unless under the direct teaching of one who knows the dangers of meddling with the psychomental apparatus of the human constitution, for dangers lurk at every step, and the meddler in these things is likely to bring disaster upon himself, both in matters of health and as regards sane mental equilibrium. The higher branches of yoga, however, such as the rāja yoga and jñāna yoga, implying strict spiritual and intellectual discipline combined with a fervid love for all beings, are perfectly safe. It is, however, the ascetic practices, etc., and the teachings that go with them, wherein lies the danger to the unwary, and they should be carefully avoided.

Yogi (*Yogin,* Sanskrit) A yogi is a devotee, one who practices the Yoga system or one or more of its various subordinate branches.

In some cases, yogis are those who strive in various ways to conquer the body and physical temptations, for instance by torture of the body. They also study more or less some of the magnificent philosophical teachings of India coming down from far distant ages of the past; but mere mental study will not make a man a mahātma, nor will any torture of the body bring about the spiritual vision — the vision sublime. (*See also* Yoga)

Yuga (Sanskrit) A word meaning an "age," a period of time. A yuga is a period of mundane time, and four of these periods are usually enumerated in "divine years":

1. Kṛita or Satya Yuga	4,000	
Sandhyā	400	
Sandhyāṃśa	400	
		4,800
2. Tretā Yuga	3,000	
Sandhyā	300	
Sandhyāṃśa	300	
		3,600
3. Dvāpara Yuga	2,000	
Sandhyā	200	
Sandhyāṃśa	200	
		2,400
4. Kali Yuga	1,000	
Sandhyā	100	
Sandhyāṃśa	100	
		1,200
Total	12,000	

This rendered in years of mortals equals:

$$4{,}800 \times 360 = 1{,}728{,}000$$
$$3{,}600 \times 360 = 1{,}296{,}000$$
$$2{,}400 \times 360 = 864{,}000$$
$$1{,}200 \times 360 = 432{,}000$$
$$\text{Total} \quad 4{,}320{,}000$$

Of these four yugas, our present racial period is the fourth or kali yuga, often called the "iron age" or the "black age." It is stated to have commenced at the moment of Krishna's death, usually given as 3,102 years before the Christian era. There is a very important point of the teaching in connection with the yugas which must not be forgotten. It is the following: The four yugas as above outlined refer to what modern theosophical philosophy calls a root-race, although indeed a root-race from its individual beginning to its individual ending is about double the length of the composite yuga above set forth in columnar form. The racial yugas, however, overlap because each new great race is born at about the middle period of the parent race, although the individual length of any one race is as above stated. Thus it is that by the overlapping of the races, a race and its succeeding race may for a long time be contemporaneous on the face of the globe.

As the four yugas are a reflection in human history of what takes place in the evolution of the earth itself and of the planetary chain, therefore the same scheme of yugas applies also on a cosmic scale — there exist the four series of satya yuga, tretā yuga, dvāpara yuga, and kali yuga, in the evolution of the earth, and on a still larger scale in the evolution of a planetary chain. Of course these cosmic yugas are very much longer than the racial yugas, but the same general scheme of 4, 3, 2 applies throughout. For further details of the teaching concerning the yugas, the student should consult H. P. Blavatsky's *The Secret Doctrine,* and the work by the present author, *Fundamentals of the Esoteric Philosophy.*

— Z —

Zodiac The Greeks called the zodiac the "circle of life," and they divided it into twelve houses or signs, named as follows: Aries, the Ram; Taurus, the Bull; Gemini, the Twins; Cancer, the Crab; Leo, the Lion; Virgo, the Virgin; Libra, the Scales; Scorpio, the Scorpion; Sagittarius, the Archer; Capricornus, the Goat; Aquarius, the Water-bearer; Pisces, the Fishes.

The entrance of the sun into each one of the twelve zodiacal constellations or signs brings with it a new cosmic force into operation, not merely on our earth, but distributively speaking throughout our own individual lives. The entering into the present astrological era which is now under way will inaugurate the development in the human race, in a certain line, of powers to come that will be nobler than were those of the last astrological zodiacal era.

There is a strict and close correspondence between each one of the globes of our earth-chain, and a respective one of the constellations of the zodiac — each such constellation being one of the "houses of the circle of life."

Index

Entry Terms are set in *italic* type, while additional terms found in the text are set in roman type. Numbers in **bold** type signify the page on which the Entry Term begins. "See" references point to related terms in the text and index.